Practical Mysticism

Practical Mysticism

Dr. Paul A. Clark

Published by the Fraternity of the Hidden Light

Fraternity of the Hidden Light

P.O. Box 5094

Covina, CA 91723

Copyright © 2015 Paul A. Clark

ISBN 9780971046955

Printed and bound in the United States by Lightning Source Press

Editing and Proofreading by Kristen Wood and Judith Ostrowitz

Cover by Joseph Sherman

Introduction: What Is Practical Mysticism?

Introduction: What Is Practical Mysticism?

Change your paradigm and you change your world. Our personal paradigm, or how we view our world, profoundly influences our every interaction. Conversely, it determines what we choose not to see. If an event or condition is in conflict with our own paradigm, we may simply not perceive it. This framework can either enhance our adaptability to change, or it may prove deadly. It provides a foundation for excellence, or may retard how we evolve into our potential.

Many people are dedicated adherents to their practice of religion. That does not necessarily make them practical or mystics. Mystics are those who are seeking a definite, direct experience. They are not satisfied with dogma, traditions, or the theoretical study of metaphysics. Rather, they seek a practice that will lead them to a numinous experience of the Ultimate. They yearn, not for faith, or belief but for a sure *knowing* of the truth of existence. True mystics know that their paradigm must be practical, because it ultimately affects their success or failure.

So, what is the life-view of the practical mystic? First, a practical mystic realizes the fallacy of placing blame or responsibility outside of herself. True, these influences can, and often do, appear to affect us. In the end, however, it is our reaction to external stimuli that dictates the outcome.

Many make it a habit to play the victim. They will say, "Thus and so made me do it," or, "I have to do this work or go to this place," or even, "The devil made me do it." The truth is that we choose either to do or not to do. We have the power of choice. But to access that power we must choose to take responsibility. If we give our responsibility away, we give our power away with it. Claim your God-given power. Does this seem mystical? It is.

A practical mystic promotes a holistic world-view that embraces everything and everyone. With the truth of personal responsibility comes the truth of *mutual responsibility*. As John Dunn admonishes us, "No man is an island unto himself." We are all centers of consciousness manifesting a profound unity. Not only are we our brother's keeper, we are our brothers and sisters. What effects one affects all. This is the mysticism of unity.

Materialists believe that the creation of life and consciousness is an accidental cosmic combination of various elements. Mystics believe that matter is never the cause of creation, but rather the effect. Matter does not create consciousness, consciousness creates matter.

The practical mystic looks forward to and embraces change.

She knows that each change is another step in the great evolutionary plan. By looking forward we become pro-active co-creators rather than reactive pawns in the great cosmic dance. Thus, we become aware of the purpose of all life. We know that we have a cosmic destiny to fulfill. We know that we are created by God to complete the plan in our own unique way.

Mysticism is intensely practical. It is a positive paradigm for growth and achievement. When we change our paradigm, we change our world. It is to aid this transformation that this book is offered.

Part 1: The Great Lies examines deeply the common delusions that affect our view of reality and life.

Part 2: The Pattern of Perfection examines, in detail, the Pattern on the Trestle Board. This powerful tool promotes our transformation into a liberated, awakened consciousness and an instrument of the Life Power.

Part 3: The Seven Stages of Spiritual Unfoldment studies a proven process handed down from the mystics of the past that leads from delusion to enlightenment.

Part 4: The Three Stages of the Adept discusses the aftermath of enlightenment.

When we accomplish this transformation, we agree with Dave Bowman when he says in *2010* by Arthur Clark, "Something wonderful is about to happen."

Part I

The Great Lies

Chapter 1: The Secret of Fulfillment

What is the secret of fulfillment? Why do some people seem ensnared in the obstacles of daily existence while others rise triumphantly, embracing and conquering challenges, to ultimately arrive at the summit of success? Time after time, these "victors" tell us that they are no different from anyone else. They report that we all have the power to accomplish our goals and realize our God-given potential.

All power exists in the moment of the present. We do not need to wait for it to appear in our future. It is already within our grasp. We just need to realize this fact, act on it, and create our destiny.

As Francis Bacon wrote, "Knowledge is Power." This power is available to everyone, at this very moment. Yet, as the world whirls through space, few are fulfilled and many are unnecessarily frustrated. Knowledge of reality differentiates these two groups. This book makes this knowledge yours.

This is powerful information. Be warned. Those who might use it for selfish advantage or to achieve personal goals by using or suppressing others will never succeed. In fact, in the end, they will end up destroying themselves. The attitude that we must eliminate the competition to attain our goals is based on lies. The knowledge of fulfillment is based on the true nature of reality—The Truth of Being.

Chapter 2: The Pilgrimage

What does your life look like? Many ask themselves the great questions without reflecting on why. Life's tests and trials have left them unhappy, mourning, and in a condition of anxiety or instability. Outward recognition and small triumphs have left them with a feeling of lack and dissatisfaction, leading them to search for the next outward "fix." Fortunately, for many, after the hard won wisdom of experience has been recognized, the silent call of the soul is received. This deep call originates within the True Self and resounds through the consciousness. It says, "Wake up. You are made for better things. You have a greater destiny!"

Still, the secret remains. The hidden, master key is undiscovered. What is it? It is simply that, "you must learn to create the space needed to receive." How is this done? It is done by giving.

This is the life-changing realization that the enlightened masters of all ages have transmitted to us. It awakens the Truth within our hearts that we may live in reciprocal harmony with all life. It prepares each of us to free our lives from the delusions of existence.

However, we must not only be willing to give, but also qualified and able. This is the purpose of this book—to present to the reader, in a straightforward manner, practical instruction on how to overcome the Great Lies, and how to attain health, happiness, and fulfillment through inner realization. This requires, on the part of the reader, the willingness to exercise the discipline needed to acquire the knowledge and techniques essential to help themselves, so that they in turn may help others. The welfare of our fellow men and women is dependent on the well-being of the individuals that make up society.

We are not separate. We are parts of the one, great consciousness. We must remember that we cannot change anyone else. It is by transforming ourselves that we will aid our own evolution and that of all who come our way, be they friend or foe, known or unknown.

To accomplish this self-improvement requires persistence, dedication, and work. Some power in the sky will not transform us. This work is personally reserved for each of us. This task, far from being hard and discouraging, is the most uplifting and rewarding process we may undertake, if it is done with joy and enthusiasm. In this book you will be given step-by-step instructions on how to recognize and overcome the Great Lies. You will learn to free your consciousness and free your true self.

Chapter 3: The Original Sins

The Great Lies

The Great Lies, also known in the Western Mysteries as "The Original Sins," are the basis of humankind's misery. They are referred to as original because they are a product of centuries old misinterpretations of experience conveyed to us through the Collective Consciousness. The Collective Consciousness is that shared memory of experience that we have in common with all humankind, present and past. It contains all of our interpretations of experience as a member of the family of humanity. These records reflect truths based on accurately interpreted experiences as well as lies based on faulty, incomplete, or incorrect observations. With regard to the Great Lies, generations on generations have reinforced these errors. As such, they are not so much acquired, as inherited. They exist as weeds in the garden of our subconscious. They are seven in number. A brief examination of each follows.

The Lie of Outer Causation

This lie states that events in our lives affect us in a random and accidental manner. It emphasizes that we are at the whim of outside forces or supernatural (divine or demonic) powers that cause us to think, feel, act, or to react to these forces. The Lie of External Causality presents man as a puppet of cosmic forces that control his responses and options from birth to the grave. When this lie is accepted, it often leads to feelings of futility and helplessness and may devastate our self-esteem by portraying man as an insignificant pawn in the universe.

In contrast, the truth is that if we consistently shape our inner world into a pattern of perfection, our outward world will manifest that pattern. Far from being insignificant, we are co-creators in partnership with God.

The Lie of Materialism

This lie states that all reality exists within the range of our physical senses. It tells us that what we see on the plane of material manifestation is the whole picture of reality, the whole truth. It is true that the physical senses can be extended by physical instruments (e.g., an electron microscope). However, this extension is still in the arena of the material.

This lie supports those systems of philosophy and socio-politico-economics that promote the acquisition and maintenance of great wealth as the primary goal for living, sometimes without regard to ethics. When one accepts this lie, it is easy to accept that the end justifies the means. It leads to conspicuous consumption and produces paranoia and undue competition-related stress, which can lead to a physical and/or mental health breakdown. The empty promise of materialism betrays even those who serve it well, leaving them spent and disappointed. In the end, they find themselves desperately searching for meaning in their lives. The truth is that only when we look within can we understand the real purpose of life and acquire those treasures that neither tarnish nor turn to dust.

The Lie of Limitation

The universe and its riches are infinite. Yet, the victims of the Lie of Limitation believe quite the opposite. They are plagued by a belief in poverty consciousness. Their operating maxim is that there is only so much good, wealth, abundance, or resources in the universe. They believe that if they do not scramble to get there first, someone will arrive before they do and steal it away. This philosophy is expressed in sayings such as, "The early bird gets the worm," or "The race goes to the swift," and "Nice guys finish last."

This lie promotes an isolation/separateness that justifies harming others to achieve one's own aim; the development of an all-consuming pursuit of wealth for wealth's sake; and conspicuous consumption—as in the former lie. When examined, this lie is based on an underlying fear of poverty and out-of-control or unchecked Capitalism. However, being rich is not the same as being fulfilled. He who dies with the most toys is still dead.

Repeatedly, if one studies the history of the human race, we find instances where new technologies and new expertise have provided breakthroughs to new riches and new opportunities. The invention of the microchip and the Internet are recent examples.

Do not make the mistake of thinking that riches or abundance are unspiritual or evil. The lie is that you must take away from others to make yourself rich. It is a historical fact that many organizations promote the idea of poverty as holy, while conspicuous examples of grandiose and exorbitant displays of wealth are evil.

The idea promoted by these organizations (i.e., that there is something inherently evil or unspiritual in abundance) is either extreme hypocrisy or a calculated smoke screen to keep the masses in near slavery. They point to scripture and read, "Money is the root of all evil," knowing, many times, that this is a misstatement based on a mistranslation. It would be closer to the true meaning of this phrase to say, "Lust for money, or greed is the root of all evil." Lust implies an overwhelming desire that causes the person who is expressing it to lose control. That is the evil.

The Lie of Mortality

The Lie of Mortality proposes the absurdity that consciousness is only associated with a physical body, specifically the brain. This lie not only promotes needless fear and grief but also promotes the idea, previously mentioned, that happiness, fulfillment, and greatness reside in the over-accumulation of physical wealth and power. It diverts us from the true purpose of evolution. It mocks justice. No vision of justice is possible without seeing the whole picture, composed of many lives, many existences. This then becomes clear that both the one who seemed to "get away with evil" and the one who was "afflicted from birth" will have many opportunities to balance the karmic scale.

In truth, our being is far vaster than these frail bodies we inhabit. We have used many bodies during many incarnations and can function away from our bodies and use inner senses that have no physical counterpart. God sculpted us in His own image in order that He might experience His creation from our unique perspectives. Our purpose is to transform ourselves into unobstructed instruments for His perceptions, and we have all eternity at our disposal to complete the task.

The Lies of Separation—From one another, From God, From Creation

Are we our brother's keeper? This lie says no, and portrays man as detached from other men, from God, and from the rest of creation. It supports the falsehood that one can gain at the expense of another. The belief that man is separate from God leads to a view of humanity as inherently weak or evil. Separation from Creation leads to the poisoning of our environment. The consequence of this lie is exploitation, crime, war, slavery, famine, and the rape of Mother Earth.

The truth is that we are one with all humankind and the rest of creation as well. When one is injured, all suffer. "Unless we all stay in the boat, we shall none of us come to shore." Within each one of us is a spark of the celestial flame. We are all children of the One Father/Mother and are learning to be clear expressions of our divine essence.

12

Summary

Here then is an overview of the original sins, otherwise known as the Great Lies. These seven delusions keep each of us in bondage and prevent us from realizing our true divine nature. We read in the gospel, "Know ye not that ye are gods?" Yet, knowing this and being aware of the obstacles is but the first step to surmounting them. "Know the truth and the truth shall set you free." What is the path to realization? What is the truth? To learn this we must explore our consciousness. The secrets of consciousness have been carefully guarded for ages by the custodians of the ancient Western Mystery schools. These are secrets that those same guardians have kept inviolate until the time was right for the awakening.

"Let the Sleepers awake!"

Chapter 4: Fear is Failure

The sage's staff struck the ground, sounding a staccato counterpoint to the pat-pat of his sandals as he moved across the desert rocks and hard-packed sand of the wasteland. His five disciples, all following in various states of discomfort, trudged a few steps behind him.

With eager anticipation, they waited for the old philosopher to utter his next words of wisdom. For the last year, the master had taught them many mystical truths relating to the principles of the Cosmos and the path to enlightenment. Still, they sensed he was, in some subtle way, dissatisfied with their progress.

Suddenly, he turned around and spoke, "Each of you has done well in study and comprehension of the theoretical basis of the great transformation. Still, there is more to treading the path to enlightenment than just thinking and studying."

He turned back around and with quick strides disappeared over a ridge. As the students scrambled to follow him, they crested the rise and then stopped abruptly. There, at the edge of a vast canyon, stood their teacher gazing at a great abyss below. He turned to them, his eyes shining with ecstasy and spoke with great emotion, "Come my children! Come see the beautiful view God has provided us!"

They looked at the old man in disbelief. Their master danced only inches from the abyss. He jumped up and down excitedly as the ground crumbled beneath his sandaled feet.

"No Master, we cannot approach. We might fall; the edge might give away beneath us. We would all be lost!"

The Sage looked at each of them with deep sadness and said, "No, my friends, you will not fall. Gather your courage and come to me. Behold the vision of the wide expanse."

The students looked at each other in shame and trepidation. "No Master, we cannot come to the edge. We are afraid."

The Sage brought his staff down sharply, sounding a gun-shot-like report. "Come to the edge," he thundered!

One by one, the five students approached the edge of the canyon and with sighs of wonder and exhilaration, stood staring at the awe-inspiring panorama.

The old philosopher quietly stepped behind them and grasping his staff horizontally pushed them all into the abyss. One by one they each grew wings and flew!

I love this story. I do not know where it originated, but it has been around for years. Many people might wonder at its point.

Therefore, let us examine it more closely, for it expounds one of the most life-transforming concepts you will ever encounter.

The pastor of the famous Crystal Cathedral in Southern California, Dr. Robert Schuller, once said, "I'd rather attempt to do something great for God and fail, than attempt to do nothing and succeed." Yet, many people become adept at attempting nothing, risking nothing that will stretch their self-concept, or anything that will provide a life enhancing experience. Why? Because they are afraid. They are afraid of risk, of failure, of embarrassment. There is an injunction in the mystical schools of the West that admonishes the seeker on this topic. It states:

> "Fear is failure. Therefore, be thou without fear.
> For in the heart (or soul) of the coward, there is no strength."

This fear is based fundamentally on a misconception of the nature of our being.

In a seminar I once attended, fear was described as **F**acts in **E**rror **A**ppearing **R**eal. Often fear is based on the wrong interpretation of data.

Take, for example, the fear of failure. There was a story circulated in the 1960's that recounts the Soviet Union's last minute attempt to beat the United States to the moon. Under the cloak of extreme secrecy, they launched their Cosmonauts into space only to miss the moon. The spacecraft's last audible transmission was "Good-bye Earth."

The hurried mission failed because their scientist's calculations proved inaccurate. The Soviets followed the formula of Ready, Aim, Fire. Unfortunately, their aim was off. A few months later, Apollo 11 landed on the surface of the Moon and made "...a giant step for Mankind." The Americans were successful because they built into their plan several in-course corrections. Understanding that their calculations contained errors or "mistakes" scientists developed a system of making corrections along the way. They followed the formula: Ready, Fire, Aim.

The point of this story is that we never suffer failure if we learn from our mistakes. Every error is a learning opportunity. The only way we can fail is not to attempt because we are afraid.

A newspaper reporter once asked Thomas Edison if his many hundreds of failed attempts to construct a working light bulb had discouraged him. He responded by saying: "What failures? I just found 300 ways not to make a light bulb." He characterized each apparent failure as one step in the process of success.

Practical Mysticism

The source of all fear is ignorance. Moreover, the root of all ignorance resides in the acceptance of the Great Lies, the Great Lies that I have referred to as the Original Sins.

Chapter 5: Delusion or Illusion

For years I lived in the San Gabriel Valley near Los Angeles. This valley is defined on its Northern side by the beautiful San Gabriel Mountains. One day I was entertaining a friend from Dallas. Walking about in my backyard on a hazy-smoggy morning he looked toward the Northern horizon and commented that the majestic mountains had disappeared. He joked that now my view was the same as the view from his own backyard in Texas. We mused that if he had visited for just this one day, the impression he would have taken back to Dallas would have been that of a flat horizon.

The seeming disappearance of the San Gabriels was an illusion. However, if my friend hadn't been aware that behind the haze there existed a range of mountains he would have suffered from a "delusion." Because of his knowledge from other days and other sources, he could see beyond the "smoke of appearances."

We are all subject to illusions or limitations presented to us by our senses. What we must free ourselves from is the acceptance that these illusions are truth. When we penetrate the veil of illusion, we emerge from the bonds of delusion, and we wake to the vision of Truth.

The Original Sins

The first bond we must break is that of ignorance. Ignorance is much more than a lack of information. It is a response to error-filled conditioning.

It has been said, "Knowing you are ignorant is the beginning of wisdom." Take, for example, the caged bird. Should it accidentally fly through an open door, it will panic and frantically attempt to reenter its prison.

Are we like the bird? Are we ignorant? To some extent, we all are. Fortunately, we have the ability to question. Like the bird, we accept misconceptions because society views these as general truth. But are they?

In Europe, during most of the 15th century, it was a commonly accepted truth that the Earth was flat and that if you sailed too far in any direction you would fall into the great abyss. During the Renaissance, the Church jailed Galileo and burned Bruno for disputing the commonly held opinion that the Sun revolved around the Earth. Many common sense truths are just plain wrong. They're delusions. Where did they come from? They originated in ignorance of the true nature of the facts. These facts were repeatedly misinterpreted due to faulty observation, which led to a deluded interpretation of reality. We, the human race, still do this today. Moreover, in the case of the Great Lies, they have been accepted for so long, and have accumulated so much energy, that most of us simply do not question them. We are like the bird that accepts its cage.

Next, we will examine the nature of these delusions and discover the method whereby their limiting effects may be overcome. These debilitating sins come to us via two channels in our consciousness. First, we acquire delusions through our upbringing, interactions with others, and our personal misinterpretations of experience. These are the lesser lies and may be corrected by realizing the truth and substituting correct patterns in our consciousness. Just as in a garden, we can cease to water the weeds and instead turn our attention and efforts to raising the flowers of correct conceptions of truth.

The second class, the Great Lies or Original Sins, are not so much acquired through our personal experience as they are inherited. No, I don't mean inherited through our personal genes like the color of our eyes or hair, but rather they are carried through the Collective Unconsciousness of the human race. We inherit them merely because we are human. They include the errors of millennia. They originated in misinterpretations and faulty observations and have been repeatedly reinforced by generation after generation of our forebears. The good news is that once we realize what they are, how they originated, and the implications of their error, we can replace them with the gold of true realization.

In the next chapter, we will examine the dynamics of our consciousness and discover the keys needed to free ourselves from the chains of bondage.

Chapter 6:   Shadows and Light

Our perception of reality is wrapped up in our concept of self. What do we mean when we say, "I am?" Most identify themselves with the personality and its fascination with the shadow play of outer conditions and events. They become so fascinated with this reflection of reality, so entranced in the drama, that they link themselves with the fiction. But who is the true watcher? We cannot answer this question until we take control and turn our attention toward the light within.

Answering this question requires desire, an adventurous spirit, and a passion to know. As the writer of the *Book of Revelation* says, lukewarm curiosity will be "spewed out!" As the legendary sage Abra-Melin advises his spiritual heir, "Enflame thyself with prayer."

When you set a goal, you galvanize all the powers of your consciousness. It focuses and gives direction to all the powers of your being. When you physically write your goal or your desire on a piece of paper, you have taken the first vital step in its realization. You have performed a truly magical act. Make your goal specific, crisp and clear and you will have begun to take control of your life and will have begun the process to free yourself from the dominance of the Lies. Because, you see, *your consciousness creates your reality.*

Materialists believe that life is the product of a cosmic accident. They tell us that we are at the mercy of mechanistic, impassive, unconscious forces that buffet us and that our only salvation is in the quickness of our reactions and the survival of the fittest.

Nevertheless, the wise tell us that these statements are based on an arrogant lie. They demonstrate the truth of their position by pointing to verifiable results. The lie that anything outside the world of manifestation ever causes us to do, think, feel, or be anything is based on incomplete observations, faulty perceptions, and incorrect interpretations of life's experiences. The so-called "real" world of the materialist is not the cause but the effect. It is the realm of conditions, appearances, and effects—the origin of which lies in the inner world of consciousness.

The source of the manifested universe is rooted in the images and consciousness residing in the thought processes of the ALL—that is, the Absolute. Humanity experiences these images and processes as the physical, manifested universe. The power that created the worlds is limitless, and is present at any point in time. Further, it is a real presence at the center of each human consciousness. This power continually expresses through human consciousness. It does not originate in you, but rather expresses through you.

You co-create with God your personal experiences of life on a moment-to-moment basis. You create your reality through the images you choose to hold and to energize with your emotions. Any clear, emotionally charged mental image will tend to materialize itself as an actual condition or event. This is demonstrable to any objectively thinking person. All one needs to do is to observe any given situation and establish a chain of causation from the past to the present. Using this process it is easy to see that our manifested reality is the result of the images we have held habitually in our consciousness.

By selecting the images that embody your goal, you will put into motion the universal creative process. When you have done this, you will make steady, sure progress towards freeing yourself from delusion and manifesting your desired reality. You will have taken the first, important step.

Chapter 7: How Consciousness Works

Our consciousness can be classified into three main modes of functioning: Superconscious, self-conscious, and subconscious. Let us examine each of these modes, how they function, and how they relate to each other. Doing so will prepare us to confront and overcome each of the original sins.

Superconscious

It is the Superconscious mode of consciousness that inspires us and provides inner promptings and intuitions. It is our inner teacher and our inner and true Self. It is the mode of consciousness that incarnated our body and constructed our personality to sojourn through time and space. The Superconscious communicates through the "still, small voice" that is always available to assist and guide—if we but take the time to listen. This mode is described by Mabel Collins in her spiritual classic titled, *Light on the Path:*

"Stand aside in the coming battle and though thou fightest, be not thou the warrior! Look for the warrior and let him fight in thee. Take his orders for battle and obey them. Obey him not as though he were a general, but as though he were thyself, and his spoken words were the utterance of thy secret desires. For he is thyself, yet infinitely wiser and stronger than thyself. Look for him, else in the fever and hurry of the fight thou mayest pass him; and he will not know thee unless thou knowest him. If thy cry meets his listening ear, then he will fight in thee and fill the dull void within. And if this is so, then canst thou go through the fight cool and unwearied, standing aside and letting him battle for thee. Then it will be impossible for thee to strike one blow amiss. But if thou look not for him, if thou pass him by, then there is no safeguard for thee. Thy brain will reel, thy heart will grow uncertain, and in the dust of the battlefield thy sight and sense will fail and thou wilt not know thy friends from thy enemies.

He is thyself, yet thou art but finite and liable to error. He is eternal and is sure. He is eternal

27

truth. When once he has entered thee and become thy warrior, he will never utterly desert thee, and at the day of the great peace he will become one with thee."

Self-Conscious

This is the reasoning, attention-focusing mode of consciousness. Western man often erroneously links his identity with this part of his personality. In other words, when the majority of people say "I," they are referring to the self-conscious part of themselves. Both the intellect and the emotions are faculties of the conscious mind. In the Qabalistic treatise *The Thirty-two Paths of Wisdom*, the self–conscious is attributed to the "Intelligence of Transparency." Something that is transparent allows light to pass through it uncolored or undistorted. Essentially this describes how the self-conscious mind of an illuminated person functions. It allows the "Light" being communicated from Superconscious to be received and transmitted clearly, without distortion, to the receptive mode of the subconscious mind.

Unfortunately, most people tend to be translucent at best and downright opaque at worst. In addition, the tendency to observe superficially and reason incorrectly is one of the origins of the Original Sins.

Some systems of spiritual development advocate clearing the mind of all conscious thought. Why would we think God would have spent tens of thousands of years evolving something of no value? What is really needed is to disassociate our identity from the self-conscious and to control it. Then it will focus and transmit the directives of the Superconscious mind to the next mode known as the subconscious mind.

Subconscious

This part of our mind normally functions below our awareness (sub–"below" and conscious–"awareness"). It controls autonomic bodily functions (e.g., breathing, heartbeat, digestion, and balance), memory, and habit patterns. It never sleeps. Moreover, it is the filter through which all perceptions, of physical and psychic origin, must pass on the way to our awareness.

The subconscious is directly linked to the Collective Unconscious; the level we share with all life below the human level (e.g., animals, etc.). This collective level is comprised, in part, by evolutionary patterns developed in earlier epochs and is often referred to as the Race Mind or the Akashic Records.

Instinct and the control of most processes in the physical body reside at this level and come to our personal utilization through the subconscious.

Since we share all thought from previous epochs of history, it is from these levels, based on misinterpretation of experience, that we derive the so-called Original Sins. These sins are weeds that grow in the garden of our personal subconscious mind.

Chapter 8: The Sleeping Giant

The subconscious, by definition, is not usually available to conscious awareness; yet it manifests in our bodies and our environment. It filters all messages from our higher or Superconscious mind, as well as the Collective Unconsciousness and the material world. It is essential to understand the way in which this part of our consciousness operates. What follows are some of the rules of the subconscious mind:

1. **The subconscious is perfectly receptive to all suggestions originating from the conscious level of human consciousness. This is the Law of Suggestion. The subconscious must be guided by the self-conscious.**

Without direction, the subconscious is selfish, amoral, and wildly uncivilized. It has no will of its own, but it is subject to inertia. The Law of Inertia, as set forth by Sir Isaac Newton, states that unless acted on by an outside force: (1) a body at rest will tend to stay at rest; and, (2) a body in motion will tend to continue in the same motion (i.e., direction and velocity). It is the second half of the definition that is most important in our examination of subconscious. The subconscious is never "at rest." In fact, this quality is necessary for our survival. We certainly would not want our subconscious "resting" when it needs to keep our lungs breathing and our heart beating.

We are continuously giving suggestions to the subconscious; we always have. And, our subconscious mind accepts every one of them—without exception. Some have more "staying power" because they carry an emotional charge. The vast majority of these suggestions, however, never manifest because they are contradicted and cancelled by counter-suggestions. The subconscious cannot choose between important and trivial, good and bad, helpful and harmful. In many ways, it is like a computer. For most of us, effectively using a computer does not mean taking it apart and examining its construction microchip by microchip. If we know how to input and retrieve information, the computer and the software will do the rest. All we must do is tell the computer what we want it to accomplish and the machine obediently pursues our wishes. However, there is one "law" of computer processing that we must observe. Programmers refer to it as "GIGO." This stands for "Garbage in, garbage out." Neither the computer nor our subconscious can make judgments on what we *meant* to say or type on the keyboard. Each merely elaborates whatever pattern has been placed into it. A computer will respond to what we input. The subconscious responds to what we feel and is little influenced by anything we may say to the contrary. We cannot lie to the subconscious about our motives.

2. Subconscious builds our bodies and modifies our environment.

To state that the subconscious builds and maintains the body is not in contradiction to the sciences of genetics and biochemistry. Hormones, DNA, and mitochondria are simply the means by which the subconscious accomplishes its job. Fortunately, we are not required to know in detail how the job is done. A baby's heart beats just as well without his understanding of cardiology. What we do need to know is how to send effective suggestions.

3. Subconscious has inexhaustible power.

The power of subconscious is limitless. It never gets tired or gives up. It is the medium through which we achieve our goals. It puts us in touch with the people and the resources needed to carry out our plans. Self-consciousness deals with the now and therefore tends to see data as independent bits of information. Subconscious correlates and sees overall patterns. Most of us have awakened from sleep with a clear picture of how several details we have been struggling with fit neatly into one coherent and understandable whole. These "Eureka" experiences are gifts from the subconscious. Whether you call it luck or synchronicity, when you have a clear image of what you want, you are in a much better position to see and seize opportunities that otherwise would have been missed.

4. **The subconscious not only has a perfect recollection of all our personal memories, but also has access to the Akashic Records or the Cosmic Memory.**

Extensive experimentation with hypnosis has made it public knowledge that even the average person never really forgets anything. All experience is stored, awaiting adequate methods for retrieving it. At the subconscious level, we are all linked, and hence, the thoughts and emotions of others can be shared. Therefore, what is known, or has ever been known, to any man or woman is within the Collective Unconsciousness and is potentially available to all humans. Often the Collective is the source of the inspirations and insights that guide great inventors.

5. The subconscious more readily accepts suggestions if they infer the desired result rather than command it.

The emotion inherent in a command is the assumption of resistance. Commands are not necessary to give instructions or make requests of someone who is attentive, eager to help, and absolutely convinced of your wisdom and authority. Since the emotion communicated to subconscious is always more effective than the words, commands (which convey the expectancy of resistance) duly manifest this resistance.

6. The subconscious responds readily to habitual actions.

A little activity every day to achieve a goal is much more effective than sporadic activity followed by long periods of inactivity. It is the predominant image that becomes manifest. Subconscious is not fooled. It responds to what is important to us, as demonstrated by repeated periods of attention.

A word of caution should be considered here. Frantic, over pressured, badgering will convey the fear of failure, not the image of success. Give calm, assured images and empower them with positive emotion.

7. The subconscious responds and communicates through symbols and pictures.

Words have little impact on the subconscious as compared to symbols, images, feelings, and actions. This is probably because the subconscious evolved before man developed written language. As a negative example: to overcome fear, if one pictured oneself being afraid and then said, "No, that is not going to happen to me," the subconscious would fail to recognize the word "no." Instead, it would work to produce the image, in this example, that of fear.

Always picture the desired result as a positive outcome. For example, in dealing with fear, imagine yourself confident, calm, and in control of your circumstances.

If say, you desire a lovely garden, you should visualize yourself walking through it, smelling the flowers and feeling the grass underfoot. Sense the warm sun and the cool shade. Hear the birds and the water splashing in the fountain. Flood the image with emotions of peace and a sustaining feeling of contentment with nature as you walk through it.

Chapter 9: Your Faithful Servant

Subconscious suggestion is maximized by ritual and ceremonial. The wise use of ceremony provides all of the elements needed to ensure a subconscious response. It is multi-sensory, utilizing visual symbols, color, chanting, movement, taste, and smell. It holds the attention on a central focus for an extended period of time.

The symbols in ritual, either archetypal or those that have been used throughout the centuries, are deeply established in the Collective Unconsciousness. Ceremonial sustains a strong emotional response. Its images conform to Cosmic Law. If performed with a properly established group, the overall effect is multiplied. The effects of group ritual are not merely additive, each individual supports and compensates for the differences in strengths of the other participants.

When working to realize goals, don't limit your options unnecessarily. Perhaps the subconscious will produce the imaged result by a means not consciously considered. Avoid allowing the conscious mind to interfere with the realm that should properly be tended by the subconscious.

A student once asked, "I have heard that a Master can have anything he or she wants. Is that true?" "Yes," replied the teacher, "The catch is, with the understanding that comes at that level, a Master only wants what is in accordance with Cosmic Law." For example, one Master said, "I have no will save to do the Will of He who sent me."

One should be very careful to choose suggestions that are consistent with Cosmic Law. No suggestion should infringe on another's freewill. The laws of Karma are all the more rigid if the debt is incurred by misuse of inner (as opposed to outer) powers. For example, if our goal is to create harmonious working conditions we should image the change in ourselves—not in our boss, our employees, or our fellow co-workers. Never should we attempt to change another without his or her explicit request. As an old Rosicrucian vow states:

> "I will attempt no direct reform in the lives of
> another, but instead will see what needs correction
> in myself, and by changing, serve as an example
> and so influence reform in others."

To attempt to change another without their consent is to stray inexcusably toward the "Dark Side." Moreover, never permit yourself to justify your actions with, "I know better than he does what is good for him." No matter how subtle, this is an attack, and it carries frightening consequences for the aggressor. To quote from the Bible, "As you sow, so shall you reap."

We all must eat the fruits of the seeds we have sown. Therefore, sow truth, harmony, growth, love, health, and enlightenment. Then you may look forward with confidence to the feast to come.

8. Once a suggestion is given to the subconscious, assume that it already is being accomplished.

This is fact on the inner levels. A well-formed and empowered image is just as much a reality on its own plane as a physical object is a reality on the plane of manifestation. The image or mental creation always precedes the manifest.

Repeated doubts will negate your positive efforts. To some aspirants, there seems to be a contradiction between "positive thinking" and seeing circumstances as they really are. True, we must recognize problems before we can solve them. We should never attempt to lie or fool the subconscious. Positive thinking is not a blind refusal to see reality and see it clearly. It is rather, the discipline of placing attention on the chosen, positive aspect of that reality. Each of us may be likened to a temple under construction. We can choose whether to focus on the outer scaffolding which is an unsightly, although necessary part of the building process, or we may place our attention on the developing beauty within. Remember, attention stimulates growth. If we focus on the weeds in our inner gardens, we will have more weeds. Focus instead on the roses and lilies, and the weeds will wither from lack of attention.

You will find that focusing on the positive is also helpful in maintaining and nurturing your relationships and is one way of helping another without infringing on his or her freewill. Learn to look behind and beyond appearances of the outer to the Essence of God developing within. Your loving acceptance will release the beauty of self that is imprisoned in immature patterns.

9. Subconscious uses deductive reasoning exclusively.

Subconscious works by elaborating a premise. It does not question the validity of the patterns self-consciousness provides. It will elaborate a false premise just as effectively as a true one. This last fact is the root of all of mankind's difficulties and is the origin of the Original Sins. While we cannot lie to the subconscious, we can and do give it false information. When we make suggestions that are founded on contradictions to truth, the elaboration of these errors is painful.

When subconscious accepts falsehoods, it manifests our lives in ways that support them. A vicious cycle ensues with subconscious delivering seeming "proof" of the rightness of the error. Self-conscious then reinforce the lie. In the next chapter, we will examine this process more closely.

10. Causality is always internal.

Mold your inner world into a state of perfection and your outer world will follow suit. Nothing outside of you is ever a cause. Rather, it is merely an effect. Statements such as, "He made me angry," or, "I am a victim of circumstances," are lies. Each of us holds the keys to our own failure or success. Bringing order to that part of the physical environment over which you have jurisdiction will help bring control to mental and emotional states as well.

11. Perfect Health is the natural state of both the Universe and the Human.

Disease is the product of stress induced either physically, environmentally, psychologically, or karmically. When you are working to heal yourself or another, you are realigning conditions with the cosmic pattern, thereby opening yourself to the power of the Universe. Moreover, subconscious does require the appropriate materials for building a healthy body. Proper food, rest, and exercise are strong suggestions for health.

Chapter 10: Mental Imagery

Once you decide to take control of your destiny and seek freedom from the Great Lies, the Cosmic will support you. Health, abundance, and fulfillment are the natural states of the Universe.

In terms of the present discussion, that which keeps you in bondage to illness, lack, and unhappiness is the acceptance of the Great Lies. Ignorance of the true relationship of our personality to Spirit keeps us in bondage. If we believe consciously in these lies, that belief is passed to our subconscious mind, which in turn, works diligently to reproduce these images as conditions of lack and unhappiness in our life. The remedy is realization of the Truth.

What is the Truth? One example of Truth is that illness is the exception rather than the rule. Good health is the rightful inheritance of each individual. True, some illnesses have their origins in karma, but *all* can improve their condition.

By embracing the truth, you can train yourself to expect health, wealth, and happiness by creating clear, dynamic images of these states. Right now, you are receiving the instruction you need—changing your mental activity will enable you to manifest the conditions you desire.

Mental imagery is a vital step. This should come as no surprise. Any work of art, be it a piece of jewelry, a painting, or a building always exists as a mental image in the mind of its creator before it manifests as a physical reality. Thus, it is important, especially in this age of ready-made fantasy and an educational system that devalues it, to take time and train our mind in this important skill. You must learn to visualize clearly and dynamically, and to convey these pictures as suggestions to your deep consciousness. Subconscious will do the rest. It will realize your dreams in your daily life.

One of the common problems encountered by students beginning this process is the inability to create clear visualizations. The decline of both reading and storytelling, combined with the proliferation of video games and their ready-made images have contributed to our current inability to produce potent images.

Still, there are some individuals, and I would hazard to guess that most of the readers of these pages are among them, who resist this trend and who seek to develop the "inner artist of their imagination." So, let us outline the procedure you will use to facilitate the process of conveying a goal as a suggestion to your subconscious.

1. Be specific. Do not be content to deal in abstracts. Whatever your goal, the realization of it will take a physical form. If your stated goal is "service," describe the specific kind of service. What activities will it involve? Who will benefit? What skills must you first develop?

 If you should want a new car, identify the exact make and type of car. Which model do you desire? What color is it? What kind of upholstery does it have? Does it have a manual or automatic transmission? Where and for what reason will you use it?

2. Remember to involve the other senses in your visualization. How does your desired car sound? How does it smell? Of what materials will it be composed? For example, a Corvette has a fiberglass body. Some cars have wooden and leather interiors. What about your dream car?

3. Make it dynamic. What movements will you make as you enjoy the achievement of your goal? See yourself in the picture–the visualization. See the image as being a present reality, in fact on the mental plane, it is already realized.

4. Write down your visualization on paper. The physical act of expressing your images and converting them into words is a very important step and cannot be overstressed. This process transforms your visualization from a hazy, vague generalization to a specific, dynamic expression of the manifestation of your goal.

Memorize the following statement of truth.

Every clear, emotionally charged, mental image will tend to manifest itself as an actual condition or event.

The act of generating a dynamic, specific visualization will energize all the powers of your subconscious and bring you the resources and conditions necessary to manifest your goal.

Chapter 11: The Secret of Creativity

Whenever we choose a well-defined goal and then embody it as an emotionally charged image, the subconscious will immediately begin its work to provide us with the connections, materials, opportunities, and people needed to accomplish it. Our efforts will invoke the great power of the Cosmic to assure its manifestation. The power that can transform the world is automatically controllable by our conscious mind provided the necessary direction is given in the correct manner.

By making positive suggestions to your subconscious mind you can not only enjoy health and prosperity, but you can also access that repository of knowledge residing in the Collective Unconscious. This vast celestial resource will provide you with all the information you need on any subject—freeing you from delusion.

We must be consistent in our suggestions. We need only observe the chaos and misfortune in the world to understand how humanity indiscriminately uses the Law of Suggestion.

Subconscious is consistently laboring to fulfill our goals. However, what suggestion are we giving our deep consciousness if our daily attitudes and behavior are in conflict with our stated goals? When we make choices and give expression to immature patterns—patterns that are inconsistent or even incompatible with our highest self-image—how will our inner servant interpret our desires? Subconscious will always and faithfully respond to the predominant suggestion. So, if our actions and attitudes give lie to our statements, what can we expect?

One of the most powerful tools in forming suggestions is knowledge. Remember, "Knowledge is power." It is therefore important to research and gather the pertinent data concerning your goal and then apply that data as needed. In this way, you are better able to harmonize your actions with your intentions.

The role of making accurate observations and correct premises falls to the self-conscious mind. Care must be taken to make sure it does its job accurately. This is especially important when we make statements that begin with the words, "I am." How often have you, without thinking, said things such as, "I am sick to death of this…" or "I'm never going to be able to afford…" and other such statements of limitation? Many of these notions of reality are embedded in the century old lies of the

Collective Unconscious. You must be vigilant to ensure that you do not unconsciously give expression to these lies and pass them on to your faithful servant, the subconscious mind.

Chapter 12: No Free Lunch

Let us correct one of the most common misunderstandings of the subconscious process. The subconscious mind may not be used to "get what you want for free."

Freedom from Responsibility

Although we use inner means to achieve our goals, we are not free from the consequences of our actions. We all know that there are consequences for the things we do. We may be rewarded or we may pay a price for our actions. In an effort to free Western man from the chains of paralyzing guilt, popular psychology has stressed that you cannot be placed on trial for what you think. This teaching is useful for the people the psychologists are trying to help. Guilt is a waste of energy—energy that should otherwise be invested in rebuilding our inner temple and our life. Additionally, those who can barely control their actions are not yet ready to take full responsibility for their thoughts. On the other hand, if you are ready to take full responsibility—for what you do, what you think, for what you feel—you may be taught how to use the intellect and emotions to make increasingly effective use of the powers of the subconscious. Does that make us exempt from the Law of Karma? Of course, it does not.

Let us use the seed and fruit analogy again. One who is untrained, undisciplined, and uses their mental imagery inconsistently will have few seeds germinate in the subconscious gardens. Thus, the plants will grow slowly. When we must finally eat the fruits of those seeds (both bitter and sweet), we often cannot remember having planted them. Indeed, the planting may not even have occurred in this lifetime. Thus, one may not see the connection between his behaviors (seeds) and the circumstances (fruits) of his life. He may feel like a helpless victim.

We all find some bitter fruits in our lives. But when we realize that they are the results of unwise suggestions planted in the past, we can learn from our mistakes and plant a new crop. With our increasing understanding of the process, these new seeds will yield results that are more pleasant. Once a person begins working effectively with the subconscious he or she becomes more aware of the seeds that are planted. When the seeds bear fruit, he must still eat of the harvest, but if it is not to his liking, he has a better chance of recognizing the causal nature of his imaging and reactions. He can, therefore, learn to plant more appropriate suggestions. The law of responsibility, which may seem oppressive to the ignorant, serves as a teacher for the wise.

It is important that we learn to consider the consequences before making suggestions to the subconscious mind. A friend of mine once used her understanding of this process to suggest to her subconscious that her baby would be born with an easy labor and delivery. She never considered the "blank spaces" in the contract. Subconscious summarily provided a very easy delivery, with no labor at all—by necessitating a caesarian section!

Freedom from Work

A novice student might assume that achieving a goal by making effective suggestions to the subconscious will render physical efforts toward that goal unnecessary. The methods outlined in this book are not an escape from work and responsibility. These techniques do not make us exempt from natural law. They teach us how to work *with* that law instead of against it to achieve our desires. The Mysteries do not support laziness. There is no better suggestion to the subconscious than physical action. We should strive a little every day to make our goal manifest. To make detailed plans and not follow up on any of them sends a clear message to the subconscious; that it is the *activity* of the planning process we want—not the manifested reality. Do something to achieve the first step of your desire. If later you decide that a different course of action is preferable, fine—modify and proceed. You may not even be able to see step two until step one is accomplished. More progress is made when we act, learn and adjust if necessary, than if we expend all of our energy planning and not doing.

We may not achieve our goal overnight. A concert pianist, for example, must practice. Physical changes will gradually occur, modifying his hands into better tools for the execution of the music. Correct imaging will maximize his effectiveness, but there is no substitute for physical effort. These teachings do not offer shortcuts, they simply streamline the process. Most people expend half their energy making suggestions that conflict with the other half. They seem to get nowhere because they have not charted a proper course and have little understanding of how to steer their vehicle. To them it might appear that those who do accomplish their goals are just lucky and are not subject to the same rules as the rest of us. However, the laws of nature and of consciousness are absolute. We all must play by the same rules. The difference is knowledge.

Chapter 13: Overcoming the Lies

When we are under the spell of the Great Delusions, we are literally seeing lies. We are accepting that which is not. Billions of people today are victims of this false vision. Everything they observe and accept is distorted and tinged by the erroneous interpretations of their personal experience and by those they have inherited from the Collective Unconscious. They look at life and its experiences through colored glasses, some dark, some rose-tinted. This does not have to be so. There is a way to overcome this slavery. There are those who are Knowers of Reality, those who see the world as it really is and find the vision beautiful.

The old mystics used the formula *solve et coagula,* which means dissolve and reform. They systematically analyzed and removed their misconceptions based on error and reformed them to reflect the eternal truth of reality. This process eliminates the volatile or unstable elements of emotions, erroneous opinions, prejudice, and personal bias that hinder our vision of life. It replaces these misconceptions with clarity of mind and body. This reformatted consciousness establishes a stable and firm foundation on which to erect the structure of new and accurate conceptions—a tower of truth built in place of the lies.

According to the spiritual teacher, Paul Foster Case, it takes about a year, if one is diligent, to purge the subconscious of its inherited and acquired false knowledge.

When this purification has been accomplished, the conscious and subconscious levels of mind are able to work together, freed from bondage, to eliminate harmful fixations. This freedom removes any built up interference or distortion of the flow of the One Life-Power.

Chapter 14: It's All Imagination

What is creative imagination? Why is it important? Creative imagination is one of the most important tools of consciousness. It actually builds the mental matrix or body that forms the basis for the manifestation of our desires. Remember, every clear, emotionally energized, mental image will to tend to manifest itself as an actual condition or event. It is this creative faculty that works out new patterns for the expression of the Life Power. It is the flow of mental substance of the deep consciousness raised and utilized to its highest role.

To gain skill in inner creativity, we must practice using this power in every conceivable way. We must use all of our skill to create a vivid dynamic awareness of the Eternal Presence which is the actual substance and consciousness of every form we perceive. Through this recognition, we gradually transform our emotional reactions to our every experience.

This change is described in the old Rosicrucian vow:

> I will look upon every event in my life
> as a particular dealing of God with my soul.

With this vow we recognize that every experience of daily life is a veil for the interaction of our life with the One Life Power. We become conscious of our inner teacher—that still, small voice of our true Self that reveals to us, through intuition, the essential spiritual quality of all experiences. Thus, we are liberated from the bondage of false judgments that lead to both repulsions and attachments.

Continually we remind ourselves to recall that, despite appearances, our everyday experiences are really the eternal activity of the One Reality. Our faith is not blind but is built on inner realization. The conviction of a practical mystic is based on the observation of eternal law. It must be established by practice and experiment and by carefully examining cause and effect.

We should not become impatient with this process. It takes time. The habit must be established, much as it does in learning any new skill. For example, a person who is learning to play the guitar must repeatedly learn to place each of his fingers on the correct strings and in the correct position on the neck of the instrument. A year later, if he has been faithful in his practice, he will automatically, unthinkingly, finger the chord and notes correctly. It takes just as much effort and practice to establish a new mental pattern. Habitual action will transfer our identification from the personality to that of one controlling consciousness. Thus, we free ourselves from slavery to the Great Lies and realize the inner essence of perfect freedom.

The *solve* part of the psychological equation, *solve et coagula*, demands that we eliminate any unwanted manifestation from the mental image of our goal. To do this we coordinate the use of our creative imagination with our power of discrimination. Then, we limit and apply concentration when defining the mental images we *do* want to see actualized. This process of *coagula* is an effective use of the Law of Inner Causation. What this all boils down to is consciously selecting the forms and images of personal activity that we energize in the manifestation of our goal, and at the same time, eliminating those that are not productive in reaching our objective.

Solidify your goal using clearly defined verbal statements and by energizing your imagination with the force of desire. See vividly what you seek to manifest, and thus, direct your emotional power away from counterproductive imagery. The process is not difficult if you proceed logically and systematically. You will eliminate indecision, doubt, and fear and replace them with patterns that express decision, courage, and confidence. Then follow up with actions that support these positive values.

Avoid wasting energy by gossiping about your hopes and goals with any who are not interested (and may, in fact, be unconsciously hostile). Remember the four maxims of the Hermetic student: Know, Will, Dare, and, Be Silent. Useless chatter diverts energy from the achievement of your goal.

Thus, we overcome the Great Lie of Outer Causation, the supposition that outer physical conditions rule our lives. The cure for this malady is simply a clearer, more conscious application of the very power that causes it. That faculty is the power of attention. When you exercise this power in a superficial way it leads to superficial generalizations that create bondage to erroneous and mistaken conclusions and opinions.

Profound observations using your power of attention will correct these mistaken patterns, which will activate your inner creativity and will, through the Law of Suggestion, lead to liberation. Remember the Law of Suggestion states:

> All levels of subconscious are completely and unfailingly amenable to control exerted by suggestions originating from the level of human self-consciousness.

Practical Mysticism

Here you will be are aided by the inertia of the collective unconsciousness, rather than being hindered by it. We must not forget that while it is true that Deep Consciousness does contain the lies and errors of the ages, it also has within it the correct interpretations of sense experience from or through the observations of the wise. The ideas and teachings of the sages of the past may be contacted here in the Akashic Library, wherein is recorded all human experience. We may picture it as a huge library full of books, some of which are authored by wise men and some of which are written by fools, false prophets and charlatans. Our understanding of a given subject depends on which authors we study. We may choose to attune our consciousness to the wise. Indeed, it is important that we do this. By aligning our consciousness to their keynote, we will gradually become one with their wisdom. Moreover, this will instill their patterns of wisdom into our very cellular consciousness. As we incorporate these maxims of understanding, we will begin building our reality on their foundation, a rock of wisdom.

This skill in separating truth from error requires we develop our ability to discriminate. We must practice disciplining the mind in the use of attention and concentration. This stilling of the "monkey mind" removes the false identification of the Self with the intellect. It is the first and indispensable step in liberation from the Great Lies. The average person's observations are often akin to a floodlight. The practical aspirant must develop his attention into a laser-like, precision instrument.

Cause and Effect

Another common mistake that most people make in connection with causation is reversing the concept of cause and effect. They feel enslaved by forces originating outside their consciousness. As the Law of Inner Causation states, causes are never external. It is we who give to these outside forces a potency they do not really possess. Subconscious, as our willing and ever obedient servant, acts on this influence and manifests our personal slavery to circumstance. Change this paradigm, and we recreate our world.

If we pay close attention to our chain of mental images, we will realize that it is our self-consciousness that is the controlling principle. The Law of Suggestion does not just work some of the time, but is the unfailing dynamic explaining the mechanics of our creative process. Once we recognize this relationship, we may gain skill through consistent, habitual practice in selecting the images we wish to activate and manifest.

Chapter 15: The Dynamics of Creation

The secret of mastery lies in recognizing and understanding the roles our three modes of consciousness play. Once we have grasped this dynamic, we may use their processes to produce our desired goals. For example, we must realize that it is our self-conscious that liberates our subconscious by freeing it from the burden of misconceptions originating from faulty interpretations at the conscious level. Aligning subconscious into right relation to the Superconscious will accomplish this. The Law of Suggestion may be utilized to create this connection.

Regardless of your gender, picture your conscious mind as a young man and the subconscious as a young woman. Imagine him grasping both of her hands in a loving, affectionate partnership. He says to her, "I hereby release you from any suggestions deriving from misinterpretations I may have made in the past. Further, any suggestions that I may give you in the future must be approved by Superconsciousness."

Now see both of them looking above to an archangelic figure, symbolizing the Superconscious, smiling down on them in approval. The light shining from the angel illuminates the woman's face. This is, in turn, is reflected to the man who gazes lovingly at the woman. (Students of Tarot symbolism will recognize that we have utilized the symbolism of the archetypal symbols found in the sixth trump of the major Arcana, known as "The Lovers." This is but one example of how these symbols may be used for a much higher purpose than fortune telling).

To further understand our three modes of consciousness we must develop our ability to concentrate. When we recognize the relationship between concentration and breathing, as Yoga practitioners have done for centuries, we may see that breath is closely related to concentration. When you actively concentrate, your breathing automatically becomes even, deeper, slower, and rhythmic. Moreover, what is normally not realized is that purposively slowing down the breath and establishing a rhythm makes concentration easier. Thus, breath control is always given emphasis in the meditative practices of both East and West.

Western culture has long labored under the delusion that the mental and the physical are two distinct and separate arenas of expression. This misconception has relegated mental processes into a secondary and even sometimes unimportant fantasy status that has forced us to deal with our environment reactively—

generally expressed as the survival of the fittest. In reality the mind and the body are different components of one integrated unit, functioning together and influencing each other. They are like two mirrors reflecting each other's images into infinity.

Self-conscious finds its primary (but not its complete expression) in the experience of the physical senses. It is the mode of consciousness that classifies and arranges the input of sense-experience. Using inductive reasoning, the self-conscious forms our theory of the nature of experience—of life. However, like a camera that is out of focus, if our observations are hazy, clouded by prejudice and superficial generalizations, our personal "picture" will not truly depict reality.

One outcome of bondage to the Great Lies is that the cellular consciousness of the trillions of cells in our body becomes programmed with these delusions. The origin of this programming, as we have emphasized, is to be found in inaccurate observations and imperfect interpretations of sensory experience—by not only us, but also those stored in the Collective Unconscious—the chains that bind us to the Original Sins. It is our self-consciousness, operating through the Law of Suggestion, by which we may free ourselves.

The role of the self-conscious mind is, surprisingly, little understood by many people who attribute to it, mistakenly, their primary identity. It is not our Self. However, it is our main interface with sensory experience and our environment. Through this level, we observe, classify, and order facts in an attempt to discern relationships and formulate general principles and laws. It is important to note that through its powers of inductive reasoning, the self-conscious mind moves from particular impressions to general concepts. It fits facts and inferences together, linking them to frame hypotheses.

From what we know of the self-conscious, it is evident that we must train ourselves in the proper use of our senses so that we may form accurate and logical conclusions. Only in this way can we apply the Law of Suggestion in an intelligent and effective manner. It is through this use of the self-conscious, including the higher centers of our physical brain, that the Superconscious influences our personality.

The Universal Subconscious

Subconscious is not a personal possession. It is the Life-Power that links all expressions of consciousness. In the Qabalah it is referred to as the Uniting Intelligence. It is this universal power that is at work and expressing in the field of subconscious.

Our body is just one of this Uniting Intelligence's infinite vehicles of expression. Through it and by it we are united not only to each other but also to all creatures expressing on levels below human consciousness. This includes the vital essence of even what exoteric science calls inorganic substance. There is no such thing as dead matter. We agree with the famous renaissance scholar and martyr, Giordano Bruno, who states that unity of consciousness is not limited to our planet or solar system. This unity extends throughout the entire universe, to the outermost reaches of time and space and to those expressions that are beyond the range of the physical.

Altering the Dynamic

All of these states of awareness are brought about by the establishment of more accurate patterns that more clearly reflect the reality of inner causation. The use of the powers of discrimination results in a balanced, stable, and equilibrated consciousness. Until this integrated relationship between the conscious and subconscious is established, there is a continual friction and lack of coordination between the two modes of mind. Once it is in place, the Law of Suggestion conveys the message of truth to our inner creator and the liberated consciousness is manifested.

Chapter 16: Overcoming the Lie of Separation

In the Chaldean Oracles, the ancient mystics urge us to "follow the river of the soul." This river is the string of associative images that our mind continuously and unceasingly pursues. We are admonished to follow these images backwards to determine the starting point of our chain of inner causation. With each link we come closer to the One Cause expressing through us. We also realize that we are not separate from each other, from the rest of creation, or from the Creator.

When we are merged with the ONE, the delusion of separation is at an end. We *know*, in no uncertain terms, that all personal actions are really performed by the One Actor expressing through us. As we become united with this ONE, we participate in its awareness of the Eternal Now.

This union does not result in the obliteration of our distinct, personal identity—quite the opposite. Through this experience we firmly establish our purified, personal identity. This definite realization of our specific identification is the objective of all mystical techniques and disciplines.

The One Creator is the spiritual essence of all. We have each been created as a unique point of experience and expression for the cosmic drama. Each of us has been sharply defined and, like a snowflake, is uniquely individual. All, from the newest soul to the most highly illuminated master, lives his or her life through the illusion of an individual personality. The master, however, realizes that it is an illusion and yet also understands the necessity of it. It is not the personality we must escape, but the delusion of identifying with it. To quote Yoga Ramacharaka:

> "The real 'I' is the Spirit principle, which is manifesting in body and mind, the highest expression of which I am conscious being myself—my soul. The 'I' cannot die nor become annihilated. It may change the form of its expression, or the vehicle of its manifestation, but it is always the same 'I'—a bit of the Universal Spirit – a drop from the great ocean of spirit—a special atom manifesting in my present consciousness, working toward perfect unfoldment. I am my soul—my Soul is I—all the

rest is but transitory and changeable. I Am—I Am—I Am."

To know the true meaning and purpose of your personality, you must be able to distinguish essence from appearance, cause from effect, subtle from gross, the I Am from its vehicle.

This "knowing" is accomplished through meditation. Regular and persistent meditation is the foundation of all mystical systems. We begin by stilling the body. Bodily stillness is the indispensable preliminary to mental quietness. We can initiate the process by concentrating on some specific object, focus, or fact of experience with the intention of establishing an unbroken flow of knowledge from that object. The result of this meditative process is the direct realization that our personality is a center of expression for the one, controlling consciousness of the Life-power.

Noted physicists, especially those in the area of Quantum Theory, have postulated that will power and light power are essentially the same. Furthermore, if the universe is one, dynamic, living organism which recent research indicates it is, then logically no part of it is separated or unrelated to any other part. The power, which operates in our cells and establishes the patterns in our bodies and consciousness, is the same power that caused the "Big Bang" and set the worlds to spin. Again, no part of the universe is unrelated to any other part. This power, which we observe at work in our environment, is a power of the One Identity, the Universal Consciousness.

Some may object that the denial of personality as our Self leads to determinism, that every activity and experience is predetermined by pre-existing causes. From the level of personality, this is perfectly correct—for most people, the personality is constantly in a mode of reaction. But spiritually aware people realize that within them is something higher, more essential than their personality, something that acts rather than reacts. This essential Self, the Individuality, is identical with the great I AM.

To become aware of our identity with the essential Self is one of the great purposes of the many techniques and disciplines of our mystical traditions. In this way we become liberated from the mechanistic laws of Karma. We move from being "at the effect" to becoming consciously identified with the cause. Yogi Ramacharaka wrote the following in his book on yoga:

> "One of the principle things indelibly impressed upon the mind by the glimpse of the higher consciousness is the knowledge—the certainty—that Life provides everything – that the universe is filled with life and is not a dead thing. Life and intelligence is seen to fill

everything. Eternal Life is sensed. Infinity is grasped. And the words 'Eternal' and 'Infinite' ever after have distinct and real meanings when thought of, although the meaning cannot be explained to others."

Preparatory Work

As a preparation for the exercises that lead to this experience in consciousness we must "stock the library" of our subconscious with those seeds that will yield productive results. For that reason the wise in all ages have encouraged the reading of sacred scriptures. We do not mean to say we should embrace these writings with the blind acceptance of the literalist, for blind faith is the attitude of an immature mind. Rather, we should study, using our powers of discrimination. Such study is an exercise of our self-conscious mind. These "revealed" or "inspirational" works echo teachings that are part of the memory of nature. They have been received and written down, but their source is in the Akashic Records.

The diligent student who compares several of the sacred writings will soon realize a common message running through all—that the Divine is a unity that has created us as personal centers of expression and experience.

71

Intellectual affirmation of the fact is insufficient. Subconscious must receive the suggestion through routinely practiced behaviors and attitudes that reflect this paradigm shift, thus remolding our world to reflect this truth.

As mentioned previously, hypnotherapists have demonstrated that we never forget any of the experiences or information to which we have been exposed. We have a perfect record in our subconscious of all the experiences of our life. By examination of this perfect record we may gain the knowledge we need to understand our particular role in the cosmic expression. We can also observe how the process of manifestation necessarily contributes to the illusion of separateness. However, we must not let this illusion transform into a delusion. Uncritical acceptance of the appearance of this lie will enslave us. We must remind ourselves continuously of the lie of separateness. We are not separate beings, but different, unique expressions of the one Life-power.

Chapter 17: Remembering Who We Are

Part II of this book examines a series of statements known as The Pattern on the Trestle Board. These statements, when used regularly as a focus for meditation, will dispel the delusion of separation and reinforce the Law of Causation.

Certain other experiences can also aid in overcoming the Lie of Separation. Most of us are familiar with the phenomena of Past Life Regression. In nineteenth century France a man by the name of Colonel De Roche carried out a series of such experiments. After placing his subjects into a hypnotic trance, he guided them stage-by-stage into their past until they reached memories connected with their birth.

He then instructed his subjects to go back further, to a time before birth. Most recounted alternate lives in different bodies. Historical records were cross-checked and it was found that the information revealed in these sessions was correct, even though his subjects had no waking knowledge of such lives.

Critics refuted De Roche's findings, believing that his subjects simply complied with his suggestions.

Yet, independent investigators found hard evidence from town and church records proving that, at the referenced time and place, the persons described during the hypnotic sessions did in fact exist. True, we may concede that De Roche's subjects may not have been remembering their own past incarnations, but the fact remains that they had accessed accurate memories of events, places, and persons that had occurred hundreds and, in some cases, thousands of years before their own birth.

While in trance, De Roche's subjects linked their personal consciousness with a vast reservoir of memories and information. Their experience was not a miracle, nor did they gain some new ability. They simply tapped into an already existing and ever present level of unified consciousness. The fact is that we are all vehicles of expression for the self-conscious level of the Life-power's activity. This revelation, impressed on our cellular consciousness, acts as a catalyst to ignite a series of bodily transformations that "re-program" our cells to express this pattern of belief. Genes do not determine this transformation—belief does! This mystical flash of reality is a participation in the One Life's complete and perfect recollection of itself. We remember, for a split second in eternity, who and what we really are.

Chapter 18: The Flash of Awakening—"Let the Sleeper Awake!"

For some, the awakening discussed in the preceding chapters can be a sudden, almost painful overthrow of our false knowledge of "the real world." I once saw an advertisement that read, "What if everything you have ever known or believed is wrong?" This momentary, yet unforgettable vision of reality is, in fact, a quick insight into the absolute truth that all life is one—a unity.

After the aspirant has experienced this "Road to Damascus" revelation, her flower of insight gradually unfolds into a grounded comprehension of the Unity of All. The realization that our specific center of experience is related to the One Consciousness of All and that the "many" are unique expressions of the All has a profound effect on our own consciousness. In its perfect knowledge, the One connects the past and the future into an ever present *now*.

We now have certain knowledge of our whole self-expression, and in turn we are known by every other part. Our personal consciousness is a specialization of the One Mind—the Life-power. It is everywhere present and all knowing. Thus, it is in constant communication with all its expressions. Each of the expressions has access to every detail of its Self-knowledge.

While we are under the influence of the Lie of Separation, we believe ourselves to have personal thoughts and feelings. We believe that our subconscious and self-conscious are personal possessions within our mind. We are told that even the greatest sages, except for comparatively fleeting experiences of ecstasy, also are subject to this illusion. They, however, know it for the delusion it is and have disciplined their minds so as not to believe in this lie.

While we struggle up the mountain of illumination seeking enlightenment, those who know, tell us that the reality is quite different from our experience of it. The wise tell us that it is rather the Cosmic Self who is gently "pulling" us toward the light. The Self that is identical with our true identity supplies us with whatever is needed at the precise moment that we need it. This means that we are destined for success and will triumph over the ignorance that deludes us. Once we realize this, we are freed from the burden of struggling to gain skill in directing and controlling a personal power that we believe we possess. The truth is that we simply need to align ourselves with the cosmic process. The universe is on our side.

Each person's liberation is part of the fulfillment of the cosmic purpose. Gradually, the One Consciousness matures our vehicles so that we can create and rule our inner kingdom wisely and in harmony with the whole.

Chapter 19: Meditation

The regular practice of meditation is a foundational part of any system of spiritual development. It is normally a four-step process:

1. Relaxation
2. Breathing
3. Concentration
4. Contemplation

Relaxation

Relaxation involves removing distractions from our environment. The practitioner should arrange a place that is as free as possible from any distracting sensory input; no bright lights or loud noise. Soft music can be played to filter out unwanted sounds. Additionally, the consistent use of the same location is suggested. With routine, the mind will associate your place of meditation with the work of inner exploration.

Relaxation of the muscles of the body is also necessary. The exotic positions of the advanced devotee of Hatha yoga require practice. In many cases, these cannot be achieved by the average Westerner without a considerable investment of time and effort.

It is better to sit in a simple straight-backed chair with hands and feet uncrossed and relaxed. How? Start with the muscles of the scalp. First tense them and then consciously relax them. Then do the same for each group of muscles until you have reached the feet. Tensing before relaxing helps to transfer tension from the unconscious to the conscious mind where then it can be systematically released.

Breathing

The science of breath is a subject worthy of an entire book. But for meditation it is better to simply rely on a deep, rhythmical breathing pattern. It should be done through the nose—both for the in and out breath. Mouth breathing should be avoided if possible. A slow breath will lead to a deep and focused concentration. The basic rule is, if you can hear your breath, you are going too fast—slow down.

Choosing the Focus

Meditation differs from relaxation in that employs a focus point. This focus may be an object, event, or concept. Often, it is defined by a question. Some have achieved remarkable success in using one of the Tarot cards as a focus. It is interesting to note that this was the original purpose of these designs.

The mind is then allowed to follow associative chains originating from the chosen focus. The meditator should be vigilant in noting when the chain drifts too far from the central subject so that he or she may gently, but firmly, pull it back to the starting point. I emphasize *gently* pull it back, otherwise, the subconscious will get the idea that we think meditation is difficult. It will then comply with this belief and become a self-fulfilling prophesy that will make our practice much more difficult. The "circling" of associative links will eventually lead to a break through to the collective levels of the One Consciousness and will provide new insights or inspirations. This is the hallmark of a successful meditation.

Contemplation

In this stage, our concentration becomes so fixed that we become one with our focus. For example, if we are meditating on the concept of compassion, we find that we become compassion.

Our daily life should provide much material for our meditative practice. Concentration on things or events in our external life should be the focus of the first stage of our sessions. Facts and experience reported by the physical senses are the foundation on which we begin our work. Special attention should be paid to circumstances arising out of our close, personal interactions—or lack of them—especially with our significant other.

The psychological attitude in which we begin the concentration stage of this work is of the utmost importance. Whatever focus is selected, we should remember that it is a starting point to link with the One Consciousness, an inexhaustible source of knowledge on our meditative subject— just as it is about all other things.

We must also quiet the mind and listen. Active listening must be in the nature of one who has awakened in the night by an unexpected sound. This expectant, confident attitude should be coupled with a firm belief that the desired information will be forthcoming, and that our consciousness will frame it in the best possible manner for us to understand and utilize it. As a result of this regular practice, the Light of Unity will dawn, and you will begin to see the Oneness of reality behind the entire manifest and apparently separate expressions of your world. Regular use of meditation will build the Temple of Oneness in your consciousness.

Chapter 20: The Bridge

At the back of the head, toward the bottom of the portion of the brain called the Cerebellum, is the Medulla Oblongata. It is from this nerve center that breathing, heartbeat, blood pressure, and other vital functions are maintained and regulated by the subconscious. In a very real sense, this part of the brain also serves as a bridge between the conscious and subconscious minds.

Remember, your cells are not mere things. They are living centers of consciousness. This consciousness is completely responsive to suggestions originating at the self-conscious level. However, even though cellular consciousness is receptive to our suggestions, we should be careful not to overly concentrate on any part of the body. When we do so, blood flow is automatically increased to that area. You can prove this phenomenon to yourself by merely concentrating on your hands and then watching them flush with color. In the case of the Medulla, congestion may occur if concentration directly on the cells is overdone. With this proviso in mind, the following technique can be an extremely useful adjunct to more conventional healing practices.

Talk to the cells in the Medulla as if they were your willing, cooperative servants. Determine the specific location of whatever cells you wish to influence. Then make your suggestion calmly and in full expectation that your directions will be obeyed. Make your suggestion concise and definite. Thus, with no more than a single suggestion per day, you will achieve your purpose.

The body carries on its cellular healing and transforming work as we sleep. Many aspirants have found, therefore, that success is most often achieved when these types of suggestions are given just before going to sleep, as we pass from the Beta (regular consciousness) to the Alpha state (the so-called waking or meditative state). If, however, you find that you keep falling to sleep before you complete your suggestion, you may want to give the suggestion just as you lie down or while sitting relaxed in a chair.

This is simply a conscious application of a natural process. It is not hard work. In fact you should find it easy. Formulate your desire in a visual form, picturing the successful outcome. Then convey that picture through your imagination to the cells of your medulla and success should be achieved.

We communicate to our subconscious through symbols and images. Thus the ability to clearly and precisely visualize our desires is vital. The exercise outlined above will modify and imprint the process in an organized way on the brain cells. This enhances the effectiveness of your suggestions.

The ability to see things as they really are, and then to clearly visualize them, as we desire them to be, is an indispensable preliminary in developing discrimination. We will then improve our ability to reason and classify our experiences according to their differences and similarities. In this way, we may judge which meditative results are helpful and productive and those that are less so.

To overcome and free ourselves from the Lie of Separation, we must firmly believe we are a center of expression for the One Consciousness. This great I AM already knows the complete truth. If we believe in the fallacy of a separate will originating at the level of personality we will continue to be enslaved by this lie. The vision of Oneness and Unity is really just seeing reality. It is neither supernatural nor miraculous. The cure of the delusion of separation is to see clearly, that, through *me*, the unfailing Cosmic Will takes form in thought, word, and deed.

Chapter 21: You are a Center of the One Life

Nature or natural selection evolved our consciousness up to this point. To take the next step, we must become co-creators with the One Consciousness. By affirming that the Life-power is ever present in our lives and that it *is* the directing, evolving, and regulating principle flowing through us at every moment, we will create a dynamic partnership with this One Self.

Self-evolution is a gradual process. It is like the purification of water by the repeated process of filtering out adulterants. Some of our cells, with their old, delusionary consciousness must be purified. Some are transformed, but many are eliminated and replaced with those of the new paradigm. These dead cells are removed from the body by the blood stream and normal eliminative functions. This is one of the reasons that all valid systems of spiritual development insist on the drinking of adequate amounts of water every day.

The ancient sages advised students to "make haste slowly." They realized that impatience sends our deep consciousness suggestions that waste our energy, create stress, and sow the seeds of failure.

The One Self knows exactly what to do at all times. What is necessary on our part is to plant the suggestion that the great consciousness is the active directing and expressing power in our lives. Then we must act from this new foundation. The transformation will be accomplished through us—not by us. Seeking this true guidance can be facilitated by taking time during the day to mentally to invoke our Higher Self.

As we develop confidence and as our understanding of the process matures, we free ourselves from attachment to the results of our endeavors. This liberates us from the anxiety to control what and how the transformation will manifest. This insecurity is based on fear and the delusion of separateness. To overcome this tendency we must remember Mother Teresa's admonition to worry not about doing great things, but to do small things with great love! Do whatever is worth doing with the intention to do the *very best you can.* This is the secret that will free you from the bondage and trap of attachment to results.

This must not be interpreted as a license to adopt an attitude of laziness or slip-shoddiness. We must do the work. We must make our goals definite and our images clear. But we do not gain heaven by force. Rather, we recognize that the One Self is achieving Its goals through us, and we resolve to participate in the Cosmic's success.

This confident reliance on the One Life expressing through us is a true recognition of the nature of will power. The ego does nothing of itself. It is simply a vehicle for the one cosmic power. Our personal plans are merely a part of the triumph of the Self.

One of the meanings of Jesus' instruction to, "become as a little child," concerns this attitude. A little child has complete confidence and relies on his parents with the utmost expectancy. Those who develop a like confidence on the foundation of the One Life will be the most receptive to the necessary inner guidance.

As has been pointed out, being in perfect obedience to natural law is the best assurance of success. The Universe is on our side. Nature is our enemy only when we oppose her. Through recognition of this fact we achieve freedom from all of the Great Lies. The delusions vanish as shadows do before the noonday sun—to the degree that we accept Divine Guidance in all aspects of our life, to that extent will we be free. Remember, this acceptance comes from within; it is not imposed by some force outside us.

Instead, if we place the origin of our power on the basis of a "personal will," we limit ourselves and our ability to achieve our purposes. However, with the revelation that we accomplish all things through us, rather than by us and when we realize that the source of our power is in the Cosmic Will, then we can fulfill our destiny as a manifestation of the One Self. With this recognition, comes, true tranquility, poise, and repose. We will truly rest our life on the "sure foundation" resulting in the attitude, earlier quoted from *Light on the Path,* of "going through the battle, cool and unwearied, unable to strike one blow amiss."

Does this mean, as some have asserted that we get rid of or ignore the rational thinking mind? Far from it—Universal Consciousness has spent millions of years slowly evolving what we call our reasoning intellect. And the cosmic neither wastes effort nor squanders any energy. All processes are unfailingly designed to produce a desired effect. Why then, we should ask these critics, would God go to such trouble to evolve an instrument that should be discarded? The answer, of course, is that they are mistaken. Once again, it is not the intellect that must be banished, but our misconception of its function and misidentification with this tool. Albert Einstein expressed it well when he wrote the following:

> "We are not alone in the Universe! A human being is part
> of the whole, called by us 'universe,' limited in time and
> space. He experiences himself, his thoughts and feelings
> as something separated from the rest—a kind of optical

delusion of his consciousness. This delusion is a prison, restricting us to our personal desires and to affection for a few persons close to us.

Our task must be to free ourselves from our prison by widening our circle of compassion to embrace all humanity and the whole of nature in its beauty."

We achieve this "widening" not as a result of throwing away our intellect, but by using our inductive reasoning logically. It comes because we seek. God will not drop it into our laps. It requires steady, dedicated, persistent practice to become conscious, unobstructed channels for the Cosmic. In fact, it is a sure sign we are approaching maturity in if we freely and joyfully undertake this discipline.

However, we must remember that it is the Lord within who does all things. We must be completely convinced that the personality does nothing whatsoever of its own. It is the Cosmic Self that is performing the transmutation and will accomplish the Great Work.

Do not disregard your reasoning mind. Weigh each concept by its dictates. Accept nothing because it is conventional wisdom or because it is seemingly inspired unless your own Inner Teacher, who is identical with the One Self, confirms it.

Chapter 22: The Inner Revelation

Hearing the Inner Teacher is an experience that confirms and permanently changes our concept of who and what we are. Critics might scoff and ridicule the mystics by saying, "Oh so now you're hearing voices." In fact, we are not hearing "voices." Instead, through the activity of the subtle hearing centers in the brain, we hear the One Voice, the voice of our true Self. We do not hear with our ears. Ears are simply modified, specialized receptors for transforming sound vibrations into nerve impulses that transmit these impulses to the hearing centers in the brain. It is through these centers that our work enables us to directly access metaphysical sound vibrations and puts us in touch with our Inner Hierophant. This inner revelation frees us from all identification with the concept of a finite, mortal self and replaces it with the absolute "knowing" that we have never been born and will never die.

Admittedly, the various disciplines or systems for mystical development outline a series of mental and physical exercises.

However, when we consistently practice the exercises and gain some degree of skill we find that we have been directed by an urging originating from our inner and higher Self. This, in fact, is the object of all our searching and practicing. Our goal is to make this contact and facilitate the realization in our lives. We should strive to deepen this conviction until we realize, as Jesus did, "I do nothing of myself. It is the Father within me who does all things." With this revelation our bodies transform into new vehicles, which cooperate perfectly with this inner direction.

This enlightenment is a revelation of the true nature of our personal life in relation to the Universal Consciousness. It transforms not only our consciousness and life but also our physical bodies. Cells are replaced with those with the impress of the new awareness. Vibrant health and vitality are promoted. Fulfilling personal relations emerge, and our ability to help others gives purpose and satisfaction to every moment. We are liberated from the spell cast by the Collective Unconsciousness and obtain guidance from the Universal Self. The dominion of the Great Lies is at an end, and we realize, on every level the, The Kingdom of Spirit is embodied in our flesh.

Part II

The Pattern of Perfection

Chapter 23: The Pattern on the Trestle Board

The Pattern on the Trestle Board is a set of concise statements of Truth about the One, Omnipotent, Omnipresent, and Omniscient Self. This is the Cosmic Self; the only Self there is. It describes how the One Consciousness of the Primal Will transforms itself, stage by stage, into the manifestation of the Cosmic in all its perfection. When we realize that this great consciousness is love, and that it is the very same principle that activates and dwells in us, we have consecrated ourselves to become an expression of the One Reality. This is the path of fulfillment—The Way of Return.

In the early 1920's, a young mystic by the name of Paul Foster Case received, while in deep meditation, a remarkable document. It was called The Pattern on the Trestle Board.

A trestle board, for those who may be unfamiliar with the term, is the table at a construction site where a copy of the master blueprints are placed—making them available to the craftsmen in the course of their work. The term, in connection with The Pattern, is most appropriate.

Paul Case had, since childhood, been gifted with clairaudient powers. He thus had access to inner teaching of a remarkable nature. This teaching took the form of instruction given through an inner voice during sessions of meditation. Early in life Case believed this inner voice to be a manifestation of his subconscious. Later, he associated the voice with someone he referred to as either "R" or "The Boss."

Case once asked "The Boss" to summarize his understanding of the ten Sephiroth on the Qabalistic Tree of Life. (Sephiroth are the major components representing the ten basic aspects of the expression of the Divine Will). The summary given to Case would soon be known as "The Pattern on the Trestle Board."

The eleven statements comprising this document are among the most profound teachings of the Hermetic or Mystical Qabalah. Yet, they remain relatively unknown and unexamined. Case's successor, Ann Davies did publish a brief commentary on The Pattern titled, *This is Truth About the Self,* in the 1960's. But, as far as I know, there have been no further publications. The present work, I believe, is the first attempt to examine this document in any detail.

The Pattern on the Trestle Board

This is Truth about the Self:

0.   All the power that ever was or will be is here now.

1.   I am a center of expression for the Primal Will-To-Good, which eternally creates and sustains the universe.

2.   Through me, its unfailing Wisdom takes form in thought and word.

3.   Filled with Understanding of its perfect law, I am guided, moment-by-moment, along the path of liberation.

4.   From the exhaustless riches of the Limitless substance, I draw all things needful, both spiritual and material.

5.   I see the manifestation of the undeviating Justice in all the circumstances of my life.

6.   In all things, great and small, I see the Beauty of the Divine expression.

7.   Living from that will and supported by the unfailing Wisdom and Understanding, mine is the Victorious life.

8.   I look forward with confidence to the perfect realization of the eternal Splendor of the Limitless Life.

9.   I rest my life, day-by-day, upon the sure Foundation of Eternal Being.

10.   The Kingdom of Spirit is embodied in my flesh.

It is recommended that the statements of The Pattern be memorized and used regularly in meditation. Thus the seeds of enlightenment will be planted in the deep consciousness of the aspirant that they may later flower forth.

Chapter 24: "This is Truth about The SELF"

This key statement of the Pattern on the Trestle Board is unique in that it bears no numerical assignment—it is all encompassing. It brings to mind two questions, questions that are of critical importance in the effective consideration of all the other statements that follow in The Pattern. Those two questions are: What is truth? Who or what is the Self?

What is truth?

Perhaps it would serve us well to analyze, Qabalistically, the concept of Truth. The word usually translated from Hebrew to represent this concept is—Emeth אמת. Breaking it down by its Hebrew letters, we have the following:

A—Aleph א, represents the Fiery Intelligence and is taken to signify the One Energy or the One Will before constraints or restrictions have been placed on it. In the Tarot it is symbolized by Key 0 of the Major Arcana—The Fool. This design expresses its ideas by showing a youth (probably Percival) just starting out on the quest for the Holy Grail. He is gazing at his goal and about to descend into the valley of experience.

Aleph is also assigned to the eleventh path on the Tree of Life—the first path emanating from the Primal Will in Kether.

M—Mem מ, the Stable Intelligence, is the mother letter assigned to Water. Thus, it is concerned with consciousness and mind because water is traditionally the symbol associated with these ideas. Additionally, the alchemists relate the symbol of water to the "First Matter," or the aspect of the creative process that acts as an intermediary between the Primal Will and Manifestation. In Tarot it is represented by Key 12—The Hanged Man and suggests, among other ideas, the truth about the creative power of consciousness. This is known as the Law of Inner Causation (examined in Part I), which states that the creative process is always initiated within the individual and that outer circumstances never dictate how this process proceeds.

Th—Tav ת, the Administrative or Serving Intelligence, is assigned to the twenty-first key of Tarot—The World. More importantly, in this context, it represents the channel or path by which the ninth Sephirah, which is Yesod or the Foundation and Astral World, pours its influence into the physical world. It therefore represents the channel through which Divine Energy moves into manifestation.

Hence, when analyzed Qabalistically Emeth or Truth reveals itself to be the constant proceeding from the Primal Source—the force behind the creative power of consciousness veiled by the appearances of the manifested world. Truth is one and is consistent throughout the creative process. It is the beacon of the lighthouse that guides us to our cosmic harbor of contentment.

Who or what is the Self?

The entire Pattern is a commentary about the Self. That is "Self" with a capital "S." It is of critical importance to reflect on exactly what is meant by "The Self." It is well known that in ancient times over the portal of the temple of Apollo at Delphi was written: "Know Thy Self." This injunction is not restricted to an intellectual quest. "Know" in the language of the Mysteries carries the connotation of unity or to become one. So the admonishment urges us to seek union with the Self. This Self is the essential You.

Many mystical students identify with only part of the personality—usually the intellect. It is natural to take pride in this part of the mind, and esotericism is a belief structure that demands intellectual development. In orthodoxy, many questions are resolved on the basis of faith or letting an authority make the determination. This is usually insufficient for an aspirant of the hidden ways. Esoteric seekers train and discipline themselves in theory, which requires mental development.

But as explained before, identifying the Self with the intellect is an error. The intellect, as part of the reactive personality, is ever shifting, fragmentary and changing. It is "shifting sand."

Generally, if you can say *my* mind or *my* intellect, *my* body or *my* personality, it is a sure indication that it is not the Self. The word "my" designates possession or ownership. Who is the owner? It is the Self.

It is the Self that is the real observer, the real *experiencer* of our lives. During the course of an incarnation, it is the Self that modifies and develops its instruments of personality so that it may more fully experience the purpose of the events in time and space.

The Self, moreover, extends its identity beyond merely one incarnation. It has been correctly pointed out that just as the personality is the vehicle for a lifetime, the Individuality (i.e., the Higher Self) is the vehicle for an evolution. Does this mean that the Individuality is the Self? If this is so, what happens to it when it has achieved the purpose of the evolutionary process? No, the Individuality is not the essential Self any more than the personality or intellect is. It is simply our connection to the True Self which inevitably may be traced to the One Identity—the One Self who created the worlds. *The Pattern* leads us to contemplate our relation to that reality. But we must remember that never, at any time or condition, is our real Self either separate from or different from the One Self.

First Exercise

In the Qabalah, the True Self is often equated with the ideas of Kether, or the Crown, which is the name of the first Sephirah on the Tree of Life. This emanation (or aspect of the Divine Consciousness) is represented by a scintillating or brightly shining globe of white light approximately seven inches in diameter (or 15 centimeters). It is visualized as resting, as its name suggests, just above and touching the head.

To intuitively realize the meaning of this first statement of *The Pattern*, the aspirant is urged to perform the following meditative exercise on at least ten separate occasions or as many times as he or she feels is beneficial.

Sit in a comfortable straight back chair, (but not so comfortable that you fall asleep). Systematically   relax each of your muscle groups as explained in Part I. When you have achieved a satisfactory state of relaxation, (this will become easier with practice) begin a deep, regular breathing pattern. Breathe in through the nose for four heart-beats; hold the air in for two heart-beats; and then breathe out through the nose for four beats. Let the breath come from the abdomen rather than the upper part of the chest. Doing so will circulate more of the air in the lungs. After you become comfortable with this breathing pattern, forget about counting the beats and just try to maintain the rhythm.

Now visualize the globe of white light above your head. Picture it the color of "sunlight on new fallen snow." As it whirls and rotates, see it drawing light from all over the universe. Maintain this image for about ten minutes.

While you are visualizing the Kether globe as clearly as you can, we will use sound to reinforce the exercise. Take a deep, full breath and intone (sing on one note with as much vibration as you can): **Eheyeh** (pronounced **Ehhh—Hay—Yeh**). This word is usually translated as "I am." Repeat your intonation three times. Visualize the vibrations of your chant echoing in the ball of light above your head.

When your chant is complete, dismiss your visualization by standing up and stomping your right foot. This should be your signal to return to normal, everyday consciousness.

Keep a journal to record any observations with this and subsequent exercises. If used faithfully, this journal will become a valuable tool to enhance your transformative growth. Keep it private.

Chapter 25:
0. "All the power that ever was or will be is here now!"

How many of us live in the present? Years ago I was preparing for a trip to Sequoia National Park. At work I had been putting in a lot of free overtime trying to complete several projects and generally "getting ahead" so that my co-workers wouldn't be swamped while I was gone, and also, so I wouldn't face quite so large a mountain of tasks when I returned.

I was just seeing the light at the end of the tunnel when, on the last day before leaving, my supervisor called me into her office and proceeded to task me with a project she had neglected. Her instructions provoked a confrontation and then necessitated me working yet another evening of overtime to finish her project.

The next afternoon, after driving to the Sierra Nevadas, I was walking amongst the majestic redwoods of the Giant Forest. The sun was breaking through the needles of the trees casting patterns of light and dark on the forest floor. Birds were serenading me, and I could hear the music of a nearby stream splashing its water on its journey toward the river. The temperature was brisk without being chilly, and I slipped into a meditative reverie as I walked underneath the protection of the great trees.

My mind slipped back into the resentment I had felt toward my boss and the unfair way in which I felt I had been treated. I replayed our argument with, "What I should've said" and then "What I would've said," and (with the twenty-twenty vision of hindsight) I, of course, emerged triumphant. Suddenly, I realized that I had returned to camp. What had happened to the serenity and the beauty of the forest? To that, because I had been living in the unchangeable past, I had been unconscious—dead. We are only truly alive when we are consciously dwelling in the present, the ever passing NOW.

In the Tarot, Key 1, The Magician, is assigned to the faculty of concentration. Not coincidently, it's assigned letter—Beth—attributed, in the Qabalistic Book of Formation *The Sepher Yetzirah*, to the pair of opposites of Life and Death. It is the ability to concentrate on the ever passing present, of living in the miracle of the moment that allows us to feel alive.

Does this mean we should forget the past or cease to plan for the future? Certainly we should not. But it does indicate that the past should not restrict the future. The future is controlled by the present. It is in the NOW that we may realize who and what we really are. It is now that we contact our true mastery. For it is now that we sit at the center of the wheel of causation.

All the power is now. There is only one power. It created the universe. We don't need to acquire or to find it. It is ours—now.

Second Exercise

This exercise builds on the one given in the previous chapter. After performing the preliminary relaxation and breathing exercises, once again establish a visualization of the Kether globe above your head. When this is accomplished, direct your attention to a space about seven inches below the base of your spine. Alternatively, you can visualize it between the feet, whichever is easier for you. Usually the choice is dictated by whether you are standing or sitting. Now visualize a twin ball of light. This one will be colored a swirl of indigo, citrine, russet, and olive green. This is your "Malkuth globe" and represents the negative pole of your cosmic battery, just as the Kether globe represents the positive pole.

As before, see the respective lights glowing in response to your breathing, but in the following manner. See the Kether center above the head increase in brilliance on each in-breath. Then see the Malkuth center (either just below the spine or between the feet) become more active on the exhalation.

After a few minutes, add the following intonations. Intone Eheyeh as before, but now alternate it with a new chant. This new chant is **Adonai** (pronounced **Ah—Doh—NAH—yee**). It means Lord.

When you chant Eheyeh, see the center above the head increase in brilliance. Then see the light travel down your back to the Malkuth center. As you intone Adonai, see this center become more brilliant. Do this for no more than ten repetitions.

Dismiss your visualization as before and write up your impressions in your journal.

Chapter 26:
1. "I am a center of expression for the Primal Will to Good,
which eternally creates and sustains the universe."

Remember, The Pattern is a series of truth statements about THE SELF. In the statement under consideration, the One Self is identified. It is the "I am." There is only one Self and we are each centers of its expression. There is only one of us. "Love thy neighbor as thy self," is not simply a moral injunction. It is a statement of a fact. It is the recognition of this unity with one another, nature, and the Divine. This unity is the basis, not only for true democracy but also for true fulfillment. Through this realization we see that all of our thoughts, actions, and emotions are the evitable consequence of an impulse originating at the source of everything. This is the primal expression of purpose of which we each are unique modifications.

The Qabalistic system known as Gematria, a discipline designed to train the consciousness in fourth dimensional thinking, provides insight into this concept of oneness.

Practical Mysticism

In Hebrew, the word for oneness or unity is אחד, AChD, *Echud* or *Achad.* By adding up the number of the letters of this word we have the following:

א A = 1	ח Ch = 8	ד D = 4	Total = 13

Therefore, thirteen is, by Gematria, the numerical symbol for unity in the Qabalah. Two other significant words in Hebrew share this number. One is אהבה AHBH, *Ahevah* (1+5+2+5) which means love. The other is בהו BHV, *Bohu* (2+5+6) which means "the void." The One Consciousness, the Primal Will or purpose is identical, in the final analysis, with love. Further, it is the void, womb, or source from which all manifestations emerge. All things, at all times and at all stages, are modifications of this impulse.

The Pattern declares that each of us, without exception, is a vehicle of expression for this One Power. Meditation on this image will yield significant results. Feelings of inadequacy and limitation will vanish.

This first statement of the Pattern also hints at the nature of creation. God does not "rest" after creation as supposed by some Western Orthodoxies. Esoteric philosophy, in agreement with modern astrophysics, states that creation is an on-going process occurring moment to moment.

Since each of us is a center for this expression of omnipotence, each of us may exercise some degree of control. What a sense of empowerment when we realize that the power of the Primal Will expresses through us and that we may choose to bless or curse this expression as it flows through our consciousness. What are the implications of this choice? The answer may lie in the words "Will to Good." The One Force, identical to love, should not be confused with "nice." Love is, in fact, the most powerful force in the universe. In reality it is the ONLY power. If we are not in harmony with this force, if we choose to curse rather than bless, we will reap the consequences. Blessing leads to fulfillment. Foolishly cursing leads to disintegration.

Third Exercise

Do the preliminary relaxations and breathing exercises, as before. Establish the previous visualizations as presented in the previous chapters. Now direct your attention to the region of your heart area. Just above and behind the center of your chest, visualize another globe of light. Picture this one a golden yellow color. See these three balls of light about seven inches in diameter. Connect the three balls by a column or tube of light about three inches in diameter.

Intone the words Eheyeh and Adonai, three times each, alternating between them. As before, see the energy moving down the column.

Now, directing your attention to the chest center, intone the word **Yeheshuah (Yeh—Heh—Shu—Ahh—ahh)** which means, "The nature of Reality is to liberate." See the globe at the chest level receive and balance the energy coming from the other two centers. The idea is that the consciousness, at the heart of your being, is the balancer or equilibrium of the forces of the Cosmic battery. Intone this word ten times before dismissing this visualization. Meditate on the implications of this concept. Record the result of this meditation in your journal.

Chapter 27:
2. "Through me its unfailing Wisdom takes form in thought and word."

We create our own experience of the One Reality on a moment-to-moment basis in accordance with the images we habitually hold and choose to energize with our emotional power. We provide the matrix of our creation through our consciousness. Does this sound presumptuous? It shouldn't, not if we remember that our consciousness is a modification of the Primal Will-to-Good.

As previously mentioned, every clear, emotionally energized, mental image tends to materialize itself as an actual condition or event. The number two statement of the Pattern highlights this fact—that the source of all of creation is the unfailing Wisdom of the One Life.

The Hebrew word for Wisdom is Chokmah and is the name of the second Sephirah of the Tree of Life. It is Sophia in Greek. It is said to be the goal of Gnosis, immediate intuitional knowledge.

Chokmah is spelled חכמה ChKMH. By analyzing these letters we may gain much insight into this second statement.

Ch—Cheth means fence or enclosure and identifies a field of activity or expression. In one sense, the human personality can be described in this way, as can the environment we create. The key concept here is that the power that finds expression in the limited field of manifestation has its origin or source in something above and superior to it.

K—Kaph, symbolized as a fist, refers to grasping and comprehension. It is related to the Law of Cycles or Rotation and to the opposites of wealth and poverty. Qabalistically, it is referred to as the Conciliating Intelligence.

The idea of rotation links up with the initial whirling nature of the Limitless Light as it focuses itself on the primal point represented by the Sephirah Kether. This is the beginning of the creative process. All subsequent expressions are modifications or differentiations of this first impulse.

M—Mem, associated with water, is assigned to the Qabalistic Intelligence of Stability and to the idea of reversal. The Wise have long referred to the one substance from which all things derive as being their "water." Water, as mentioned previously, is commonly a symbol for consciousness because consciousness behaves, in many ways, like physical water. It moves in currents, has tides, assumes the form of any container

114

holding it, and dissolves forms placed against its current. This water is what the alchemists refer to as The First Matter. It is the One Substance that comprises all forms. We must train ourselves to become receptive to the flow of this "water." Then we may *consciously* direct the form it takes.

H—Heh symbolizes a window. When placed at the beginning of a word, it is the definite article "the." At the end of a word it carries the meanings of "definition." Hence, this letter is assigned to the Constituting Intelligence in the Qabalah. It is also related to the Zodiacal sign Aries. This sign is ruled by the planet Mars and relates to the meanings and activities of Will.

What does this analysis of the letters of Chokmah reveal to us concerning Wisdom? First, Wisdom is not so much a quality to be actively sought but instead it is something to which we must become receptive—to flow into our field of awareness. It is interesting to note that the root of the word Qabalah, (Qebel) is the Hebrew verb "to receive," hence Qabalah is often referred to as "the received tradition." We cannot attain Gnosis through our intellect. It is an experience of Grace. But we can facilitate our reception by preparing ourselves for the experience. The personality prepares the vehicle but the Individuality or Higher Self bestows the illumination. Symbolically, the Ace of Cups in Tarot depicts this realization by representing the Holy Spirit as a dove descending into the chalice.

Secondly, we must firmly grasp the concept that the mental substance is real and not an abstraction. It is from this Prima Materium that all physical manifestation springs. We give it form through our imagination. It is by our understanding of this substance that we build our universe.

Wisdom is not something that can be realized intellectually—is a realization that dawns from within. The universe reveals (literally unveils) this aspect of truth to us. In this respect, it is interesting to remember the old mystery adage:

"I am Isis. No man has lifted my veil."

Isis reveals herself to those who have trained themselves to receive her Wisdom. This revelation gives form to our universe through our mental concepts—our images expressed through our words and thoughts. These become the matrices of creation. Imagination is the vehicle of manifestation. It is imperative that we learn to direct it in Wisdom, consciously and consistently.

Fourth Exercise

To perform this exercise it will be necessary for you to familiarize yourself with the design of Key 1, The Magician, of the Major Arcana of the Tarot. Use either the Case B.O.T.A. or the Waite Rider version.

After you are acquainted with this key to the extent that you are able to visualize it with your eyes closed, proceed with the following technique.

Start with your relaxation and breathing exercises as you have done for the prior meditations. Visualize yourself as the Magician of the Tarot. See the wand lifted in your right hand, drawing the power from the spiritual realms above and flowing through you into your downward pointing left hand and into the garden of manifestation below. Consider that all of your power originates from the One Source and that you are a channel for its beneficent expression in all of the forms of your sphere of influence. "See" it flowing through you like a stream of pure water. Bless it as it flows out into the world of manifestation. With this thought in mind, take a deep breath and chant, ten times:

Ab Aimah (Pronounced **Abba—A—Yah—Mah—Yah**)

Please note: All "A's" in this chant are pronounced short, as in Ahhh. This chant is a combination of two Hebrew words. The first is the word for father and the second is the word for mother.

Practical Mysticism

You are therefore symbolically aligning yourself with the balanced forces of the masculine and the feminine.

Close your meditation as usual.

Chapter 28:
3. "Filled with Understanding of Its perfect law, I am guided moment by moment along the Path of Liberation."

This statement is a commentary on the third Sephirah of the Tree of Life, Binah, or Understanding. It is referred to in Qabalistic literature as the Sanctifying Intelligence. The word, sanctify, means to make pure or holy. It is similar in meaning to the word consecrate.

Two more attributions connected with Binah are naturally important in this connection. First, this Sephirah is located on the Tree of Life at the head of the Pillar of Form. Secondly, it sits on the side of the Tree attributed to the future and the Divine Feminine. But perhaps more than this, the aspect of the One Power at the level of this third Sephirah emphasizes a major principle that is often expressed in the literature of the Western Mysteries. It is the task of purifying our consciousness, of making it "holy" (i.e., whole), and this can be accomplished only in the world of manifested form. It is while we are in human incarnation that we must complete the Great Work. With all the talk of higher initiations and the like, we still must prove our realizations and hone our responses here in the manifest. Aleister Crowley is famous for his admonishment:

"Do what Thou wilt be the whole of the Law."

On the face of it, many have interpreted this as an injunction to narcissism at best or licentiousness, at worst. I think there is a deeper meaning he meant to convey. The word Thou is a technical term in the Qabalah associated with the Sephirah Kether, seat of the Yekhidah or Indivisible Consciousness and the Primal Will. So when Crowley urges us to seek, discover, and give expression to our True Will, it is an injunction to align ourselves with the perfect Will of the Cosmic. Jesus said much the same thing, when he stated:

"I have no will save to do the will of He who sent me."
And again:
"Not my will, but Thy will be done."
And finally:
"Thy will be done on Earth as it is in Heaven."

These statements reveal the same truth. There is but one will in the Universe and that is the Primal Will of the Cosmic

Source. We express free will only to the extent that we are able to align with this One Will.

Crowley further identifies the nature of this power, this Will, when he states:

"Love is the Law; Love under Will."

Once again, do not the writings of the Christian New Testament tell us that, "God is Love?" The essence of the One Creative Power, the One Law is Love—Love as it is expressed on all levels. Love as an expression of unconditional, unrestricted, unselfish recognition of the unity of all life.

Recognition of the unity with the One Source guides us to the purpose, moment by moment, to the goal of true liberation. This is liberation from the fear of failure, inadequacy, and ignorance.

Fifth Exercise

In this exercise, once again we will be using the symbolic imagery of the Tarot. Place before you Tarot Key 0, The Fool,

and Key 9, The Hermit. After completing your preliminary relaxation and breathing routines, look intently at these cards.

121

After ten minutes of contemplating their symbolism, close your eyes and picture yourself as the Fool. Feel the sun shining on your back. Hear the dog barking to you in cheerful companionship. Feel the weight of the satchel and rod on your shoulder. Finally, feel the adventure of the quest, the journey.

Next, notice that as you walk along the path, the sky becomes darker and darker. The wind starts to blow, and you find yourself in the midst of a storm. The dog crowds close to your legs and whimpers. You are afraid that you are lost.

Suddenly, from the mountain peak above, you see a beckoning beacon of light. In a flash of lightening, you see the Hermit smiling down at you and shining his lantern to light the path before you. He shouts words of encouragement. Your courage and confidence returns; your dog, barking happily, runs ahead to greet his old friend.

Take a moment to reflect. Know that when life seems dark and foreboding and you feel lost, if you turn within and hold out your hand, trustingly seeking help, guidance from above will always find you.

Chant the following ancient invocation to the light:

Holy art Thou, Lord of the Universe!

Holy art Thou, who nature hath not formed!

Holy art Thou, oh vast and mighty one!

Lord of the Light and of the Darkness!

Close your meditation as usual.

.

Chapter 29:
4. "From the exhaustless riches of the Limitless Substance, I draw all things needful, both spiritual and material."

Have you ever wondered what it would be like to have an unlimited line of credit at the bank? Imagine how it would free us to achieve things that, normally, we would never attempt.

As I write these words, the phrase, "would never attempt" echoes repeatedly in my mind. A wise man once said, "It is better to attempt great things and fail, than to attempt nothing and succeed." Fear is the herald of failure. When we inhibit ourselves, with the paralysis of fear, we cut ourselves off from the omnipotence, benevolence, and riches of the One Source. This is an act of self-restriction—it is our delusion. Even the Bible affirms that it is God's good pleasure to give to us the riches of the Kingdom.

The truth is that the only power that can limit our access to the exhaustless riches of the Cosmic is the power of our belief. The Limitless Substance is always flowing through us, moment-by-moment. It is closer than hands and feet. It is instantly responsive to our images and beliefs. It is our source, and that source is the infinite.

We restrict it when precedent binds us. When we allow the incomplete and inaccurate misinterpretation of past experience to determine our future, we find that our access to our rightful inheritance is stolen by the thief named fear.

We are destined to fulfill our birthright—that of complete expression of the One Spirit. This source will unfailingly supply us with everything we need, both spiritual and material. Whatever we need—we already possess. All we need do is to realize this fact.

The universal substance is infinite. Modern physics has postulated that at any given point in time and space, we should be able to access an unlimited source of power. They call this The Zero-Point Field. Day-by-day scientific discovery comes closer to confirming what Ageless Wisdom already knows to be a fact. Are you ready to believe?

Sixth Exercise

Perform the customary preliminary exercises.

Visualize a central globe of radiance in your heart region. See it bathed in bright golden light. See it pulsing in time with your heartbeat. Now visualize a stream of golden light connecting this center with the sun of our solar system. See it as linking you directly to the spiritual consciousness of this great daystar. The physical sun is the manifested form of a great consciousness that is similar in type but different in degree to our own awareness. Feel this union. With every in breath, see your personal heart center glowing and growing as it receives the flow from the sun. Soon, you find that you are completely surrounded by and at one with this great, radiant star. You are the center of consciousness for this light. Let your radiance increase until it fills your surroundings. Let your intention be to heal and harmonize all who are touched by your radiance.

Intone the syllable **IAO** (pronounced **Eeee—Ahhhh— Ohhh**) ten times. Feel the "exhaustless riches of the Limitless Substance" flow through you to nourish, to heal, and to enlighten all those within your sphere of influence.

Let the image slowly fade as you return to normal consciousness. Remember to write an entry in your journal for this exercise.

Chapter 30:
5. "I recognize the manifestation of the undeviating Justice in all the circumstances of my life."

I find it interesting to observe that this statement often provokes feelings of unease in aspirants. Perhaps it is in reaction to the "divine boogey-man" promoted by the image of the vengeful deity in the Old Testament, other myths, and probably a lot of parents. But further meditation on this statement reveals the comforting concept that the reality of Cosmic Law governs the way the Universe interacts with each of us.

The idea of a capricious God or Goddess, a wrathful cosmic tyrant replete with all of our human shortcomings in control of our destiny *should* evoke feelings of insecurity and anxiety. Fortunately, these images are the product of an immature consciousness.

The truth is far more sublime. The Law of Karma is the manifestation of a benevolent, guiding consciousness that is consistent and present throughout the Universe.

In the Ancient Egyptian mysteries Justice was served by weighing the candidate's soul against the Feather of Maat, the

Goddess of Truth. During this ceremony, forty-two assessors or judges would challenge the initiate to explain his or her actions in life. A frank, in depth self-examination of one's conduct was required. Yet, the success or failure of the candidate hinged on the verdict of the forty-second and last assessor who asked the question: "Is there anyone who was glad that you have lived?"

In other words, have we made a difference for the good? We are reminded of the classic Christmas film, "It's a Wonderful Life," where the protagonist is shown the misery that would have occurred if he had not been born.

When we become overwhelmed with the concepts of original sin and unworthiness, it is good to remember also "original blessing and godliness."

Karma is not a punishment. When Jesus was tempted in the wilderness, it was the spirit that tested him. It was by facing and passing those tests that he emerged victorious. If there are no tests there is no triumph.

The expression of Divine Justice in our lives helps us realize where we have "missed the mark" in past actions and patterns. By careful observation we may make course corrections to ensure that we are moving closer to our goals of self-fulfillment and enlightenment. As Reverend Ann Davies once wrote in her booklet, *This is Truth about the Self,* "Understand that we have all been reaping our own immature pictures. You can now change these pictures closer to the heart's desire."

The Seventh Exercise

Perform the preliminary relaxation and breathing exercises as described in the earlier lessons. When this has been accomplished, build the images of the globe above your head, below your feet and in your heart area. Now add the image of a globe in the area of the genitals. This globe represents all your subconscious patterns, including those inherited from the race consciousness. With each breath see the center in the heart glowing brighter and passing this brilliance into the globe representing the subconscious.

Intone three times the Divine name attributed to Kether, (**Eheyeh**). Now intone the name connected with Malkuth, (**Adonai**), also three times. Proceed with the divine name for Tiphareth, (**Yeheshuah**), three times. Finally, chant the name "**Shaddai El Chai**", (**Shah—die—eeee—el—Ky—eeee**), associated with Yesod, three times.

Meditate quietly for a few minutes. Acknowledge the energy you feel in your body, and then let the images fade. Close with the usual procedure. Write about your practice in your journal.

Chapter 31:
6. "In all things, great and small, I see the Beauty of the Divine Expression."

There is One Life and One Law expressing in the creation of the universe, the spin of galaxies, the revolution of planets, and the dance of subatomic particles. Wherever we look, we see evidence of this fact.

When Rene`Schwaller de Lubiz conducted his decade long study of the Luxor Temple in Egypt, he was surprised to find that the builders of that sacred edifice demonstrated knowledge of the geometric proportions known as the two great irrationals, popularly supposed to have been discovered at a much later time by the Greeks. These mathematical proportions are known as *Pi* and *Phi*. The first defines the relationship of a circle's diameter to its circumference.

Of greater interest, for our purpose, is the second. This proportion is sometimes referred to as the golden section or the extreme-mean proportion. It is symbolically depicted by the pentagram, used by the ancient Pythagoreans as a recognition symbol.

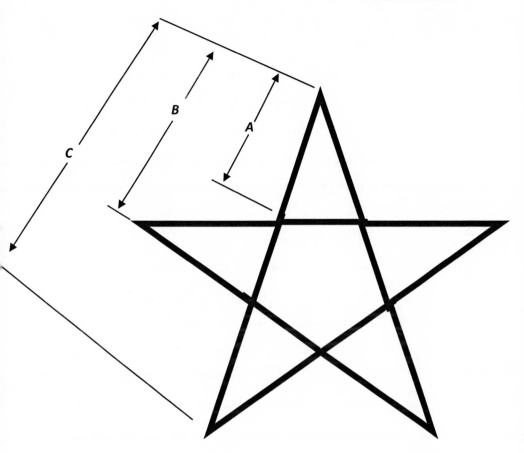

In this diagram, A is to B as B is to C. Described another way the lesser (A) has the same proportion to the greater (B) as the greater portion (B) has to the whole (C). Philosophically this expresses the important relationship:

Nature is to Human Consciousness

as Human Consciousness is to the Divine.

The extreme-mean proportion is the foundation for the famous Fibonacci Sequence (1,2,3,5,8,13,21..). Any number in the series is the sum of the two preceding numbers. For example: 3+5=8; 5+8=13; 8+13=21; 13+21=34, etcetera. The Fibonacci Series has been discovered as the foundational basis in the construction of, trees, seashells, and much more. Most impressively, it is in evidence in the distances between the Sun and the orbits of the planets. Wherever scientists and mystics look, great or small, they see the beauty of Divine Manifestation.

Beauty, or Tiphareth, is the name Qabalists use to designate the sixth Sephirah on the Tree of Life. It is the middle or fulcrum point of this diagram. It is referred to as the Mediating Intelligence. It is also assigned to the Higher Self and the Divine Spark in human consciousness. In this way, the Qabalists point out that it is the role of human Individuality to act as the mediator between the divine and the manifest. This is most evident in manifestations that exhibit beauty, and beauty is evident at all levels. Thus we see the Divine Plan in all aspects of creation

Eighth Exercise

Perform the following visualization:

"I find myself floating comfortably in an abyss of warm darkness. Slowly I become aware of a spark of light in my heart. This spark pulsates with my breath. As I fix my attention it grows in both intensity and size. Suddenly, I recognize that I have become a star. I now notice a lump of cold, dark matter circulating about me a short distance away. Intuitively, I recognize this as a planet. It is cold, lifeless, but full of potential. I am moved by compassion and by love to send out a ray of life, warmth, and blessing to this lifeless rock. I watch in amazement at its transformation. It becomes, warm, green and full of life, all because of the power of love. I return my consciousness to my normal, everyday functioning and close my meditation. As I write my experience in my journal, I pay special attention to the connection between love and life, and how they manifest as beauty."

Chapter 32:
7. "Living from that Will, supported by Its unfailing Wisdom and Understanding, mine is the Victorious Life."

We derive our existence from the Primal Will. The power that flows through our consciousness is identical to the energy that set the Cosmos into being. Its power is limitless and to the extent that we align with this great Consciousness, we are assured of success. Its law is based on the harmonious, equilibrated interaction of the Supernal Wisdom and Understanding. Meditating on this interaction as it is depicted on the Tree of Life will provide many illuminations.

The activity of Supernal Wisdom and Understanding on the Tree of Life is revealed by the Sephiroth Chokmah and Binah and the reciprocal 14th Path of the letter, Daleth.

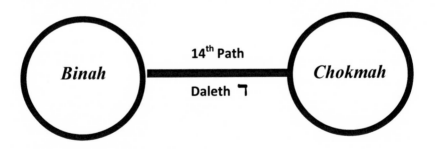

Chokmah is considered to be the expression of the projective energy of the Divine Father. It is the ecstatic energy of the Primal Will. The Chaldean Oracles describe it as that "Fountain of Insupportable Brilliance" that hurled the universe into expression with a "reechoing roar."

Chokmah is also assigned to the first letter of the Tetragrammaton or Holy Name of God. This is the letter "Y" (**Yod** ') assigned to the element of fire, which is often compared to the seed or sperm.

Balancing Chokmah on the other end of the 14th Path is the Sephirah Binah. This Sephirah is attributed to the Cosmic Mother energy. This, of course, can be seen to balance or equilibrate the male energy of the Sephirah Chokmah. While Chokmah is force, Binah is archetypal "form." It has been called the cosmic, nurturing womb.

Binah is also known as Amah, which translates as the dark, sterile, terrible mother expressed in Kali and the other mythological dark mother figures. This forbidding figure is transformed into Aimah, the bright, fertile mother represented in mythology by Ceres. The transformation symbolically occurs by the addition of I (**Yod** ') the seed. Thus Amah (**AMH אמה**) becomes Aimah (**AIMAH אימה**). She is made fertile by receiving the seed of the Cosmic Father. The channel for this union is the 14th path assigned to the letter D **d**, Daleth and the "Luminous Intelligence."

The letter Daleth is assigned to the planet Venus. Venus is associated with love, creative imagination and, perhaps most importantly to the universal desire force.

In *Light on the Path*, we are counseled at one point to "kill out desire." Yet, to eliminate desire is to effectively kill out aspiration, evolution, and spiritual fulfillment. Desire is the gasoline that powers the engine of aspiration. However, if we read further in the book we find that the counsel refers to desire for *things* and it urges us to desire fervently *illumination*.

All motivation, all achievement, all triumphs and victories of the spirit are based on a fiery desire that is Divine in origin. True, many times it is difficult to discern the holy source of this impulse. We see it distorted, twisted, and many times perverted. But, like the Devil of the 15th Key of Tarot, beneath the caricature of life, is veiled the Light of God. It is our task to seek it, strip away the veils and cleanse the lens of expression so that it may shine clearly into our life. This requires us to be diligent in the selection of the channels of expression for our sacred desire. No longer can we relegate this holy power to the gutters. We must lift it up, and by doing so, it will lift us up into the Divine Victory.

Ninth Exercise

Prepare yourself as usual by relaxing and using the breathing techniques. After achieving the desired state of relaxation and breathing rhythms, see yourself floating in an immense womb of warm, velvety darkness. All around you is comforting, nurturing, protective night. In the distance, you now see a ball of scintillating, sparkling light. It whirls and pulsates. All of a sudden, you see it explode outwardly as a spark of brilliance. In a circular trajectory, this spark is irresistibly drawn to you. It penetrates your aura with a feeling of cosmic ecstasy. It penetrates to your very heart. Suddenly you feel as if you have all the energy you need to manifest your heart's desire. You feel compassion, love, unlimited power, and wisdom. The spark begins to beat in time with your heart.

Now take a deep breath and chant **Ahhh-ooo-mmmm** three times, remembering to take a deep, complete breath for each repetition.

Now bring yourself back to full physical awareness and record in your journal the impressions you received while in this meditative state.

Chapter 33:
8. "I look forward with confidence to the perfect realization
of the Limitless Light."

Success is already assured, but fear can delay its realization. Fear implants patterns of insecurity and failure into our consciousness. Our deep consciousness then fulfills these images—images of failure.

We must reject these pictures of insufficiency suavely, gently, but firmly. To reject and attempt to eliminate them with great fanfare and energy is counterproductive and only serves to reinforce their power. Instead, we simply acknowledge that they are based on error and then reaffirm the truth of the riches of the Limitless Light.

We have the cosmic right to succeed. It is our destiny. Nothing can thwart this. But, as has been explained, we can delay its fulfillment. The choice and the power are ours. This is the firm foundational stone of confidence.

"Perfect love casteth out all fear." So to seek the perfect realization of the Eternal Splendor, we must first realize and express the power of Love. Love is a divine potency that is present in every aspect of creation. We only have to open ourselves to it. To do this requires courage; the courage to realize we are enough; the courage to remember that we are worthy; the courage to express the realization that we are loved; and the courage to act on these realizations. Yet Love is not only a noun—it is also a verb.

I was recently attempting to pull out of a parking lot into traffic. Because of an unexpected quick change of the traffic light, I found myself stuck in the driveway. As I waited for the light to once again change, I noticed a sixty-something, short, stout man walking towards me vigorously, shaking his head side to side. I could see he was muttering to himself.

When he got close enough, I could see that I was the source of his displeasure. He stopped and proceeded to "chew me out." As the words, largely unintelligible, poured from his lips, I was able to garner two bits of information—three actually. One, I should have stopped behind an imaginary line about eight feet behind where I now was located. Two, I had committed the unpardonable sin of blocking *his* way on *his* sidewalk. And, three, I was an idiot, a jerk, and worse.

I responded to his words with a truly enlightened remark; something about where in his anatomy he could place his comments. He continued down the sidewalk, a little faster, still shaking his head. I started to laugh and then stopped, reflecting.

How easy it had been for me to slip into that mass-mind reflex. It is easy to love the lovable and easy to be brotherly to those who are being nice to us. How much more difficult it is to love the unlovable. Even though, as Mother Teresa once expressed, these are our "Christs" in disguise.

I then remembered a story I had heard about Dr. Lloyd Ogilvie, the famous minister. The story goes that one early Sunday morning, when the faithful had arrived at their downtown, large, and prestigious church, they found a surprise. Passed out in an alcoholic stupor on the front steps of the church was a foul smelling, raggedy old drunk. Each of the churchgoers carefully stepped over the odiferous individual, making sure that they did not come into contact with his offensive person. The church filled up as usual; but just as the service was about to commence, just as Dr. Ogilvie was about to enter and preach, lo and behold, who should come staggering down the main aisle but this same drunk. Evidently he had decided that he was going to attend services—at least it was warmer inside. The congregation was aghast. The ushers and the deacons didn't know what to do. Should someone go tell Dr. Ogilvie and get instructions? To the horror of all, the drunk walked down the aisle to the very front, continued to the altar rail, climbed the steps, and situated himself behind the pulpit. Finally, to the members' astonishment, he removed his dirty, stained hat and looked out at the congregation.

There, dressed in rags, stood Dr. Ogilvie. He looked at each of them and said, "You may be able to guess what my sermon is for this morning. It is 'What you have done for the least of these'…"

It requires little effort to love the lovable. The test comes when we encounter those miserable souls who seem to infect everyone around them with their unhappiness. Can we love the unlovable? Can we treat, as Mother Teresa did, every one of these difficult people as if they were our Christ in disguise?

When we can do this consistently, we then have prepared ourselves to see the Eternal Splendor of Life. We will have learned the secret—not attempting to do great things, but to do small things with great love.

The attitude of confident expectation is critical in the quest for perfect realization. To doubt or to fear is to predict failure. To look forward with confidence is to realize that the goal has already been achieved.

Chapter 34:
9. "I rest my life, day to day, upon the sure Foundation of Eternal Being."

For the materialist, life is a continual race. Their motto, "the unexpected happens," subjects them to needless stress as they strive to outguess the next random event in their day.

I often ask my fellow students to play the, "What If?" game. I urge them to consider "what if" their most cherished beliefs were in error. What if there is no existence after bodily death? What if there is no Justice, no Good and no Love? What if there is no God? What if…?

Amazingly, nearly everyone answers the same way—that they would still live their daily lives exactly as they have. That a life's worth of behavior and attitudes based on the eternal values of justice, goodness, love, and eternity is sufficient reward in and of itself—whether or not God is watching.

Yet, for those who have not contemplated their motivational values, when thrust into the arena of daily existence the, "…dust of the battlefield fills their eyes," (*Light on the Path*) their "senses reel and they know not their friends from their enemies."

They have built their house on the sand, and it will surely shift during the storms. They need a foundation—a rock on which to raise their personal temple.

Fortunately, the Truth is not based only on the faith of the religionist. It is founded on observable, verifiable, cosmic law. This law is known as *Inner Causation* and, once again, it may be summed up in these words:

> We create our experience of the universe on a moment-to-moment basis through the images we habitually hold and choose to energize with our emotional power. These images form the matrix of manifestation and are continually fed to our deep consciousness. It is this consciousness that creates our reality.

When we purify our habitual response patterns and encourage them to reflect the Truth of cosmic Principles, our lives rest on the sure Foundation of Eternal Being.

Tenth Exercise

Begin your breathing and relaxation exercises as usual. When you have achieved the desired state of mental readiness, let these images arise in your consciousness:

Picture yourself standing on a sandy beach at the seashore. Consider for a moment that the water of the ocean represents your deep, inner consciousness, sometimes called the Subconscious mind. The land may symbolize the objective world of manifestation—the world of physical form.

Direct your attention to the place where the sea and the land meet. Notice it is not fixed, but varies, in flux from wave to wave. Yet, there is a pattern, a cycle to this movement. Watch the waves as they crash on the shore, melt into the sand, and then retreat invisibly beneath the surface of the beach. Each wave seems to have an identity, but in reality each one exists as part of the ocean as a whole. Each retreats into its greater expression after accomplishing its journey to the land.

Sometimes the wave leaves a gift on the land, a piece of wood, a shell, or, perhaps a starfish. Reach down and throw the stranded starfish back into the ocean, giving the gift of life back to the sea. Note in your journal those gifts from the ocean of inner life that have been given you, and return the gift with some of your own expressions of the unity of all things

Chapter 35

10. "The Kingdom of Spirit is embodied in my flesh."

A considerable portion of Jesus' teachings in the Christian Bible deals with what is known as The Mysteries of the Kingdom. He advises, "Seek ye first the Kingdom of Heaven and all things will be added to you." Most of his parables describe this "place." But is the Kingdom really a location? Certainly not, for he tells us, "The Kingdom of Heaven is within." It is, therefore, a state of consciousness. And, as we have noted in the previous lessons, our experience of the world we live in is largely, if not completely, dependent on our state of consciousness.

"Be ye in the world but not of it!" What is the inner meaning behind this Biblical injunction? Is "the world" really the enemy? For millennia the orthodox religions of the West have preached a doctrine denigrating abundance, material riches, the physical body, and the physical world. They exalt as virtuous the qualities of poverty, denial, and asceticism. This is especially curious when we look at the extravagant show of riches gathered around the practices of the same religious organizations.

Aside from keeping the common man in a state of servitude, what effect does this mistaken attitude have on the group mind of our civilization? It has led to a critical separation in our Collective Consciousness on several levels. It has fed the Lie of Separation, the lie that we are separate from each other—the "better me than thee" syndrome. It is untrue that we can ever benefit at the expense of another. When one suffers—all suffer. When one struggles with ignorance, it affects us all. The lie that we are completely isolated and unrelated has led to war, famine, and crimes of violence against our fellow humans.

Just as humanity is one, there is no separation between humanity and nature. The earth is not merely a thing for us to use. The Lie of Separation has led to the rape of the environment, resulting in deforestation, acid rain, pollution of our water supply, and global warming. These trends will have fatal consequences if not corrected. We are the stewards, not the consumers of nature.

The third implication of Lie of Separation is perhaps the most insidious because it prevents us from establishing a self-identity that will enable us to correct any of the three aspects of this lie— the lie that we are separate from God. We are not the result of a cosmic accident. Separateness from God robs each of us of our divine nobility and worthiness. The Qabalah asserts the sacredness of the manifest universe, describing it as the luminous garment of Adonai. Malkuth, as the fruit of the Tree, is the fulfillment of the pattern of perfection, truly the "Kingdom of Spirit is embodied in my flesh."

Part III

The Seven Stages of Spiritual Unfoldment

Chapter 36: Spiritual Unfoldment

Paul Case, in his writing on the Seven Stages of Spiritual Unfoldment as revealed in the Tarot Keys of the major arcana, emphasized Keys number 15 to 21. These designs are profoundly useful in awakening the spiritual seeker to the wisdom of each of these phases of spiritual development. Additionally they aid in creating the psychological and physiological changes that transform the aspirant from common Homo sapiens into a new, illuminated being that I have chosen to call "Homo Adeptus." In this section, I've attempted to outline the factors that distinguish each of the stages so that the thoughtful, dedicated aspirant may have a road map to use on his journey on the Path.

Chapter 37: The Bondage of Ignorance

The Life Power always knows what it is doing. It is omniscient. So the aspirant may find it strange that the conditions of bondage and ignorance characterize the first stage of unfoldment. But understanding their nature provides the impetus to change. By studying these qualities and our reaction to them, we may learn much about how the universe works.

As was pointed out in the discussion of the Lie of Materialism, causation is always internal. Creation is an interior process that manifests as an outward condition, state of mind, or an event. It is the establishment of a finite definition or restriction to produce a desired result. For example, if you want to build a chair, you might go through the following mental process. Let's start with the idea of "sitting." We decide that a piece of furniture to aid this activity is needed. Let's build a chair, but what kind of chair? There are many types, each suited for a unique purpose: garden benches, easy chairs, captain chairs, and desk chairs, to name a few. What kind do we want? For what purpose do we need a chair? Let's say we want an office chair. What style? What material do we prefer? How about the color or style? Each choice excludes or restricts other options. This is the way consciousness works. Ignorance, fear, and bondage each have their place and function. They are not contrary to cosmic law. They are phases or stages of the process, the method through which the Cosmic operates. This process of concretization is an inevitable consequence of the descent of spirit in to the arena of expression of "Name and Form."

The perception of limitation is a state of imperfect expression of our self-conscious mind—a mode of consciousness evolved to deal with time and space. It finds its primary expression in the interpretation of the physical universe, or sensory experience. But this is not its complete expression. Through the observation of facts and phenomena, it classifies and makes generalizations of the data of sensory experience. Functioning inductively (i.e., making generalizations from the observations and analyses of many data sets) builds a large system of theory. The danger is that quite often these generalizations are based on hasty, superficial, incorrect, or insufficient evidence. This results in a misapplication of the principle of limitation and a restriction of the powers of our consciousness.

151

When these false generalizations are accepted by our analytical mind as being a true interpretation of experience, they are planted like a seed in our deep mind. Remember the Law of Suggestion, which states that our subconscious mind is completely, and without reservation, amenable to suggestions transmitted to it by our self-conscious mode. When these suggestions are received by the subconscious, it works using deductive reasoning and manifests the misperceived data to its logical conclusion. Reasoning deductively from a wrong premise results in a wrong conclusion. Our subconscious computer does not have the power of critique. Thus, it is of the utmost importance that the potent suggestions of our personal interpretations of experience be as accurate and complete as possible.

Subconscious is truly our inner creator. It determines the structure and functioning of our subtle vehicles. Yet, as we have pointed out, it lacks the power of discrimination. It works out conclusions from the generalizations given to it from the self-conscious level based on the latter's perception and interpretation of sensation. If these interpretations are wrong or inaccurate, they will, in accordance with Cosmic Law, produce conditions of ignorance and bondage. This state is not a punishment from God, but rather, the lawful outcome of these misinterpretations as accepted by the collective consciousness of the trillions of cells in our subtle and physical bodies. These mistakes must be purged from these cellular patterns. To correct this situation we do not meddle with the functioning of the subconscious, but rather focus our attention on correcting the imperfect observations and inaccurate interpretations of our sense experience.

However, as was expressed in the earlier sections of this book, these misinterpretations are not all the result of our personal, inaccurate interpretations. Much of this incorrect or incomplete information originates in the errors we inherit from the Collective Unconsciousness. These race memories are combined with our personal faulty observations to form the patterns that limit and bind us to this stage. Yet it is also these patterns that often provide the impetus to start the inward journey of unfoldment.

This first stage of unfoldment is intimately tied to the test of the Lie of Materialism. This is the mistaken acceptance of the material is the only "real world" and the supposition that outside physical circumstances determine our life situation. Thus, we imagine that we are the pawns of forces operating on the plane of the manifest. Many, who may profess to be on the spiritual path, preach the highest ideals, believe in a life of chaste austerity, and still live under the delusion of outer causation, living their lives in bondage.

Like an algebraic equation, the solution to our delusion of bondage and ignorance lies in examining the problem itself. The cure for this limiting pattern is an accurate exercise of the very activity from which it originates. When we learn to observe more accurately, more profoundly, our inductions will reflect reality more precisely. The subconscious will then make accurate generalizations that will work through the Law of Suggestion and free us from bondage. As scripture promises, "The Truth will set us free."

These new mental patterns, serving as the matrix for creation will begin to transform our bodies, and the effect is cumulative. Once we start the process, our subconscious will impress the new, liberating patterns on the consciousness of the new cells. As noted in a previous chapter, the existing cells that cannot adapt to the new liberating consciousness will be replaced. The ones that already hold the wise information from earlier suggestions will be awakened into new activity. We will find our minds intuiting wisdom that we had long forgotten.

To initiate this process we must first learn to properly concentrate. We must penetrate the veil of illusion erected by our faulty observations and behold the truth hiding behind it. As an aid to the exercise of this concentration, it is recommended that we pursue a course of study that will assist in replacing the past misinterpretations with truths based on the inspiration recorded by the wise thinkers of the past. Books written by illuminated teachers of the past, religious or philosophical, poetry or prose, will provide our subconscious with the needed suggestions to access the memory of nature and the patterns that will lead to our liberation.

Remember, the Life Power, the Cosmic, knows exactly how to accomplish the process of Self-awakening. It is a Unity expressing itself through an infinite number of individuals. It will work through us to free us from the chains of bondage and ignorance. But we have to do our part. Intellectual acceptance is the beginning, but it is not enough. We must put our convictions into practice. Use every method that comes to your mind to remind yourself during your daily activities that you are a center for the expression and a manifestation of the Limitless Life. Use The Pattern on the Trestle Board. Memorize these statements and meditate on them daily. Remember and remind yourself who and what you really are.

Take care to make conscious, accurate suggestions to your deep mind. Conscientious vigilance will reveal how often we fall back on the Lie of Outer Causation. Remember, causes are never external no matter how often or how much it seems we are affected by our environment. Outer conditions do not affect our inner consciousness, and it is this inner consciousness that creates our universe on a moment-by-moment basis. Do not play the part of the slave to circumstance. Your self-conscious mind controls your creative powers through the power of suggestion. Reverse the suggestion of bondage and you reverse the consequences. Reaffirm that you are in control and that you are an expression of the Cosmic, expressing as the unique expression of you.

Persistent practice of remembering and affirmation are some of the most powerful tools in overcoming these lies seated in the race consciousness. Mistaken patterns and interpretations can be overcome and their consequences rectified if you practice daily to implant suggestive seeds in your subconscious garden. Soon you will reach a critical mass and the cellular consciousness will tip the scale in favor of liberation. Then you will find your environment responding in harmony with your images of freedom.

Chapter 38: What if Everything You Know to be True is Wrong?

It has been said that the only person who looks forward to change is a baby with a wet diaper. But it is a fact that you cannot reach illumination unless you change. Change is uncomfortable unless, of course, it provides a release from pain. Perhaps this is the reason that God built pain and suffering into the cosmic plan. When we suffer, we draw nearer to those who have suffered before or with us. Suffering is the spoon that hollows out the cup of compassion. It is a motivator for change.

Change is scary. It is human to desire that which is known and comfortable. It has even been said, "Better a devil you know, than one you don't!"

Paul Case named the second stage of spiritual unfoldment, "Awakening." It is at this stage we awaken from the dreams of delusion, whether they are pleasant or nightmares. It takes courage to boldly look into the darkness, and then, when the lightning flash of insight illuminates it for just a second, to see and accept what it reveals.

For what if everything you knew to be true turns out to be based on a lie? So, you have to ask yourself, "Do I truly want to be liberated or am I satisfied with my comfortable prison?" If you decide that you want to be liberated, then read on.

We discussed in the last chapter what we must do to facilitate this awakening process, this liberation from bondage. We must seek our inner guidance, taking a little time every day to listen to the inner voice of our Self. Pay attention to the voice of your own insights. Write them down and examine them. Are they logical, reasonable? They should be. Perhaps we did not recognize them until they were revealed to us, but once our inner teacher has given us them, they should appear self-evident. By writing them down, we are giving our subconscious a powerful suggestion that here is important information. Pay attention!

So choose a time you can keep on a faithful basis. Any time will do, so long as it isn't too near bedtime or too soon after a meal. At both these times you will tend to be sleepy and inattentive. Choose a place where you will regularly meditate and will not be disturbed. Thus, this place and time will tell your inner consciousness that this is a sacred exercise.

Relax, take some cleansing breaths, and flex and relax your muscles to get rid of any unconscious tension. Then formulate the subject of your meditation in the form of a question. Ask the question of your inner teacher and then wait quietly for the answer. Expect it. It will come. Listen actively, expectantly, not passively. As I have said before, listen as if you had awakened in the middle of the night, alone in a house that you knew to be empty—but you have just heard a sound downstairs.

Some, who are naturally somewhat psychic, may actually hear a voice. But others may just get a feeling. Whatever form it takes, write it down. By doing so, you will anchor the message to the conscious mind.

Do not be discouraged by revelations you feel are rather mundane or do not have cosmic import. Like all new disciplines, your skills will build with time. You can be certain that your inner teacher, your own intuition, will give you appropriate answers for your current stage of development.

While the first stage of unfoldment primarily works through the mode of the self-conscious mind, the second stage utilizes the subliminal (below the threshold) mode. This aspect of our deep consciousness has perfect access to the Collective Unconsciousness. It has been demonstrated repeatedly that it has perfect recall. Nothing is ever forgotten. Through it we may come to realize all knowledge necessary to fulfill our unique potential, our particular expression of the Cosmic.

Remember, whatever seems to be our particular patterns of consciousness is really an expression of the Universal

Consciousness expressing through us. As The Pattern on the Trestle Board reminds us, "Through me its unfailing wisdom takes form in thought and word." Thus, the feeling of personal separation is an illusion. However, this illusion, which is a necessary by-product of the manifestation process, should not become a delusion. By continually reminding ourselves of this fact, we imprint this truth on our subconscious. When we do this often and consistently, we reach a critical balance that will free us from the delusion of separation and bondage.

By careful observation using the powers of our conscious mind, we may see the dance of the cosmic, "The beauty of the Divine expression" is in all things great and small. By careful use of our senses, we discover that all outward play in time and space is really the action of a single unity of Being. This discovery is transferred to our deep mind where it acts as a seed that will grow and awaken our consciousness from bondage, limitation, and ignorance. By accurately observing outer plane phenomena, we provide subconscious with the facts for accurate inductions based not on wishes or dreams but on reality.

This stage of unfoldment first takes the form of an intellectual comprehension of the unity of life. Later, as the consciousness is transformed, we shall experience it directly.

The experience of awakening cannot be scheduled. It will come "like a thief in the night." Weeks, months, or even years patiently working on these changes may need to occur before the experience is manifested. The slow transformation progresses at the level of subconscious until, all at once, the aspirant experiences a flash of awakening. This direct perception may be very dramatic, overturning the comfortable but false delusions of the past.

Sometimes physical symptoms will even accompany the event. Remember the story in the Book of Acts where Paul is struck by a flash of light while riding on an ass on the road to Damascus. Paul's transformation was so sudden and intense that he suffered temporary blindness. His story is not merely symbolic, but describes a real experience that in extreme cases may temporarily paralyze one of more of the senses. Even if these physical symptoms are not present, the psychological disorientation of the stripping away of the veil of delusion can be so pronounced that the aspirant may temporarily think he has lost his mind. The experience is only temporary and no seeker is subjected to it until their higher mind has prepared the personality to withstand the shock. While the event may seem sudden, it is really the culmination of an orderly series of changes and adjustments made in the aspirant's mental and physical constitution.

The experience of awakening alters the seeker's perception of reality. Never again will she fall under the delusion of separateness. She will have experienced, first hand, the truth of the unity of all being. Even though, with time some of the details of the vision may fade and, at times, the illusion of bondage and separation may see to close in again, the fundamental change in the consciousness of the seeker is permanent. She has awakened. She knows the truth and this knowledge will sustain her in her journey toward ultimate cosmic consciousness. She has become one, if only for an instant, with the omniscience of the ALL. This knowledge has transformed the essence of her personal consciousness.

The aspirant is now different from her fellows. She is no longer subject to the Lie of Separation. The innermost reality of her being is revealed, and she finds that we are each immortal agents of expression of the great consciousness. We are all centers of expression of the ALL, and it is our destiny to be part of the cosmic plan.

In the next chapter we will discuss how our inner teacher provides us with knowledge to continue the process.

Chapter 39: Contacting the Teacher Within

After the field of consciousness has been laid fallow and the stress of the Awakening has occurred, there comes a time of gradual calm adjustment. The flash of illumination has passed and has freed us from the delusion of separation and the bondage of ignorance. Now we must allow the inner consciousness to replace the old worn out patterns with the new patterns of true perception. It is a period of gradual growth and revelation in stark contrast with the dynamic and sometimes painful experience of the overthrow of the false ego. Gradually, quietly, during this stage of unfoldment, we begin to receive teaching and guidance from the Teacher Within.

This third stage begins with a period of re-evaluation. We find that the "truths" of the world that we thought we knew while deluded by the old worldview, were based on error. We rebelled against a perceived enemy that bound us with the chains of restriction. But now, we see the purpose of limitation and use it to create liberation. By disciplining our power of concentration we guide it into channels that create beautiful and fulfilling forms of expression.

We accomplish this through the practice of meditation. Through this discipline, we open ourselves to contact the ever-available wisdom that is the basis for the transformation revealed in the third stage. What is meditation? Is it just sitting and trying to think of nothing? Must we hum a mantra or nonsense syllable? The great Raja Yogic Sage Patanjali wrote in his classic, *The Yoga Aphorisms*, that meditation is the continued flow of knowledge from a selected object. Thus we may understand that meditation is, in reality, prolonged concentration.

Other adepts of this practice have told us that when we meditate correctly, we find that, surprisingly, it is not we who are meditating, but rather it is we who are being meditated. We participate in a cosmic process that flows through us. In the mystical traditions, it is stated that since the One Cosmic Life Power is omnipresent, then it logically follows that it is a living, conscious presence in each of us. We are expressions of the One Power, the One Consciousness, which set the universe into motion at the instant of the "Big Bang." With effective meditation practice, we simply become aware of this fact—that our personal consciousness is a specialization of the Cosmic Consciousness. Through this point of unity we have access to all knowledge contained in the Infinite Consciousness.

Under the influence of the delusion of separation, it appears that we each have a separate, distinct self-conscious and subconscious. This is normal, but it is an illusion. Even the most evolved masters and adepts share in this illusion. True, as we have pointed out, in the brief periods when they experience the highest spiritual ecstasy, this veil is temporarily lifted; but the illusion returns. Yet there is this one significant difference. Those who have this experience never forget it. They know that this feeling of separation is a delusion and even though the feeling of separation returns, they are not fooled by it. They KNOW they are one with the Cosmic.

This realization acts as a potent suggestion to your subconscious. Instead of acting from the premise that the knowledge you need to access will be through arduous, personal effort, approach it as an agent or expression of the Divine Knowledge. Assume that you already have the required information within you. All you must do is transform yourself into a transparent channel.

Select any particular subject or object as the focus for your concentration. State your inquiry as a clear, definite question. Focus on it, and expect a reply. Be patient, like a fisherman waiting for the fish to bite. When you get the answer, write it down and act on its implications.

The Cosmic already knows the answer. It knows just what information you need—even before you ask it. Our subconscious, which contains all of our memories, is one with the Universal Unconsciousness. This Cosmic memory has complete knowledge of every thought that humankind has ever had, including the mysteries that resided in the library of Alexandria, the forgotten secrets of the East. As the Bible advises us, "There is nothing that shall not be revealed unto you."

However, the correct practice of meditation yields results beyond that of mental knowledge. It imprints the cellular consciousness with the new patterns of fulfillment that will lead to unfoldment.

In both the Eastern and Western Traditions, we find the age-old doctrine of bodily subtle centers where the vital energy is transferred for use by our physical organism. This is the basis for acupuncture, Reiki, Qi Gong and pranic healing. This doctrine also is traditionally important in yoga, alchemy, and most traditional martial arts. These centers are called chakras in the East and are referred to by Western mystics as the inner holy planets. While not accepted as yet by the materialistic scientists of the West, research is slowly adding evidence of the validity and acceptability of these doctrines. For example, a large study recently revealed the effectiveness of acupuncture, and many health insurance providers now cover it as a legitimate treatment.

Proper meditation synchronizes and balances these inner centers. It aids in the sublimation of the force known in the East as Kundalini.

While continence and chastity are requirements for spiritual development, celibacy is not necessary. The doctrine of celibacy is rooted in repression and the attitude that sex is evil. Extreme suppression actually becomes a hindrance to the transformation process by passing to subconscious the suggestion that the energy of life is somehow unspiritual. A proper attitude and healthy living are indispensable preliminaries to attainment. Control, however, does not mean suppression.

The belief pattern that sex is unspiritual is rooted in the errors of the past, when the idea that sexual union became tied up with the ideas of conquest and control. This misconception must be replaced with the concept of sacred sex. The act of union must be viewed as a sacrament that elevates the partners and becomes an expression of love and intimacy. Until aspirants replace the deluded patterns of separation with the right understanding of the sex function, the false doctrine will enslave them.

Two fundamental facts will build the foundation for this transformation. First, the sex force is manifested as the drive for reproduction only on the material plane of expression. It has other planes of expression as well, including emotional, etheric, mental, and spiritual. Second, spiritual or sacred uses of this great

167

power for illumination may be hindered by either repression or by excessive use for purely physical satisfaction. As always, the right path lies in moderation and attitude—the middle way.

In this third stage of unfoldment, the practice of right meditation modifies the nerve force ordinarily employed during sexual reproduction. It does not however employ techniques that alter the sexual act. It releases and lifts up the Kundalini or "serpent power." This subtle nerve energy is stored at the center located at the base of the spine. It may be raised to energize the higher centers in the brain. However, the serious student should avoid the practice of direct concentration on these centers to hasten this process. Through correct meditation, the Cosmic will gradually, safely, and automatically modify this nerve energy and raise the Kundalini in a safe manner.

As a result of persistent and regular practice of correct meditation you will begin to awaken to the unity veiled by the appearances of the external world. This will become clearer as the veil is penetrated and your realizations become deeper and more profound. You will perceive the patterns behind appearances, and you will witness the cycles of Cosmic Law.

As your practice deepens, you will gradually begin to shift your personal identity from the ever-changing shadow play of the personality to identification with the great consciousness manifest in nature. You will begin to see how your personal consciousness is intimately linked to the cycles embodied in the manifested universe. You will realize that the outward world before you is the "luminous garment" of the Divine. This is the planting of the seed of truth that will lead to the birth of the experience of non-separation, of Unity. All of our mental and emotional states are specializations and manifestations of the Cosmic, just as the waves that break on our beaches are one with the great currents of the ocean. You will know that, in truth, you are a center of consciousness for the primal power that created the universe and continues to support its existence right now.

In the first stage of unfoldment, we become aware of the illusion of bondage. During the second stage we awaken suddenly to the realization of the nature of truth. This awakening initiates the process that will eventually lead to the illuminated human being. In the third and fourth stages, a gradual transformation occurs that slowly and surely changes the seeker from an ordinary person to one that is an expression of the conscious realization of the oneness of all life. As Paul Foster Case once wrote, "It isn't necessary to intellectually monitor or even understand the physiological details of this transformation. Just recognize the fact that it is taking place." Indeed, the correct attitude of the aspirant should be that of a witness to the work of the Life.

Chapter 40: Transforming Yourself

A basic understanding of human physiology will aid the conscious mind in implanting powerful suggestions that will transform the seeker. Let us start by examining the basic divisions of the brain. We have three main parts: (1) The Cerebral Cortex; (2) The Limbic system, and; (3) The Central Core.

The Cerebral Cortex is devoted to the higher mental functions, such as problem solving and creative activities. It is located toward the front and top of the cranium.

The Limbic system, made up of the hypothalamus, hippocampus, and amygdale, primarily functions as an organizer of habits, memory, and some autonomic functions such as blood pressure, heart beat, etc.

The Central Core, sometimes called the reptilian brain, contains the pons and the m*edulla oblongata. The medulla controls breathing, chemical equilibrium, and most other vital functions as mentioned in Part I. Mystics have known for ages that through this part of the brain, we may contact the race memories contained in the collective unconsciousness. Memories that stretch back to the beginning of the evolutionary journey. This part of the brain also serves as the directing center that replaces old worn-out cells with new ones. Through the use of visualization, we may directly impress our suggestions of new liberated patterns of spirituality on these cells. We will thus program our cells with the imprint of truth that will help us overcome the lies of past misconceptions. When we bring these new cells under the control of the self-conscious mind, we may greatly facilitate the illumination process. The assumption that these new cells will communicate and influence other cells in their groups to adopt the concepts of liberation and mastery is a powerful suggestion. This will tip the balance at a critical point where the entire organism will be transmuted.

In chapter 20 we "spoke" to our cells through the medulla in order to overcome the Lie of Separation. Here we will utilize a similar procedure.

Prepare yourself for meditation as usual and then focus on cleansing your vehicle.

After ten to fifteen minutes, clearly formulate the intention of programming your cells with a new pattern of truth. See the image being transferred directly to the cells of your medulla oblongata in the lower, rear section of your brain. Have an imaginary conversation with the cells. Explain carefully through images and words what it is you wish to achieve. Your subconscious will be receptive. Your cells will cooperate with you. They are centers of consciousness and are eager to comply with the new patterns. Speak to the specific cell group you wish to imprint. The medulla will act as your intermediary. Remember to remain calm and self-assured which will invoke the Great Law of Suggestion.

You don't have to beat the cells into submission. The subconscious is ready and willing to cooperate. In fact, if you over do it, or if you use too many repetitions, you will communicate the suggestion of doubt. For this reason, only perform this practice a maximum of once a day. As mentioned before, the best time to do this work is just before going to sleep. Thus, your subconscious mind will work on the suggestion at the same time it normally works to heal the body, at night, during sleep when the conscious mind is in abeyance.

We are working with our body-consciousness, what the old mystics use to refer to as the Corporeal Intelligence. It is the consciousness that is concerned with the maintenance activity of the cell groups of your physical body. It is an awakening to the fact that the physical universe, our bodies included, are the products of universal consciousness. This realization comes as a result of proper mental activity. We learn it in the 3rd stage of unfoldment. We put it into practice during this 4th stage.

This activity, as a quick review will reveal, is based, in a large part, on our ability to clearly visualize. To effectively visualize we must be observant. We must be able to see things as they really are. Hasty, incomplete, and inefficient observation, leads to faulty conclusions. Correct observation and classification of data must be acquired before any real success in this practice can be achieved. When we see clearly, we begin to observe patterns and will classify this data into accurate inductions.

Nature has evolved the human species up to this point through natural evolution. But to fulfill God's plan we must become co-creators. As we begin to understand and cooperate with this process intelligently, we will progress more rapidly. We are assured of success. Once our feet are placed on the Path, the completion of the journey is guaranteed.

The Life power is not impersonal. It is an intimate, daily presence in all that we do. This great consciousness, as we have said before, is omniscient. It understands clearly and completely every principle involved in the intricate process of Its self-fulfillment. It is centered in each one of us—in you. William Shakespeare wrote, "Know Thy Self and to Thine own Self be true," summing up the purpose of life.

During this stage of unfoldment we begin to experience the intimacy of the great divine consciousness dwelling within. It expresses itself uniquely as each one of us. Through the cells of the spiritual centers located in our brain we realize that: The Kingdom of Spirit is embodied in our flesh.

Chapter 41: The Secret of Regeneration

The 5th stage of unfoldment is often referred to as the work of Regeneration. This title literally means, "to be born again." Do not confuse this with the claims made by exoteric religionists. It has nothing to do with their doctrine of being "saved from eternal damnation." However, it is intimately connected with Jesus' admonition to become a little child. Through its achievement we begin to regain the "first day consciousness," that spirit of awe and wonder that is the hallmark of the truly enlightened. Gone is the cynicism and jadedness that characterizes a deluded outlook of the world.

The fruition of this stage of unfoldment carries the realization that the cosmic self-conscious mode of the universal will is the power that is expressed in all phases of personal self-consciousness. As The Pattern on the Trestle Board states, "Through me its unfailing wisdom takes form in thought and word."

In mystical terminology, this self-conscious level is referred to as The Transparent Intelligence. When our personal consciousness is functioning in an enlightened manner, it is transparent and allows the light of Universal Truth to pass through it unimpeded. When it functions in less than ideal form, it colors and distorts the higher realizations with its prejudices and ignorance.

The power to "clean the window of perception" is now unfolding through us. This evolutionary journey is bringing our particular aspect of the cosmic plan ever closer to realization in our awareness. As we continue this process of becoming transparent, it may seem that this is of our own initiative. We may feel that, by our individual effort, we are continually seeking to work in harmony with the universal law. Consciousness, however, is not a personal possession or attribute. We remind ourselves that we are part of the cosmic continuum and use this information to seed our subconscious with the proper suggestions.

The Life Power is omniscient and connects to all expressions of the universe, including organic, inorganic living and so-called non-living. This directing intelligence is progressing toward a positive fulfillment of that Cosmic destiny that guides and directs us along the path of liberated consciousness. This process of unfoldment will develop our mental instruments to enhance our ability to clearly, concisely, and accurately express our understanding of the universal plan.

During the 5th stage of unfoldment we reacquire a simple, child-like view of daily existence. This wonder-filled vision of creation is what is referred to in the mystical tradition as "first-day consciousness." It is the recognition that we are the witness to the miracle of creation and that all events, all things great and small are expressed through us. We become aware that we are the children of God, and that all things and events meet within us to work for the Good to accomplish God's purpose and to fulfill His plan.

Chapter 42: Risen from the Grave of Error

In the 6th stage of unfoldment, we emerge into the truly mystical. We move from the consciousness of the three dimensions of the manifest world (height, width and thickness) to center into the awareness of the dimension of consciousness. This doesn't mean that we no longer exist in or deal with the material universe. We don't step into a parallel universe. Rather our perception of reality changes.

Much of this change is linked to our concept of time. We normally view time by dividing it into past, present and future. These qualities are based on spatial orientations, in other words our perception of the outer, material universe. Thus we are dealing with effects instead of causes. A day is conceived to be the time it takes for the Earth to complete one rotation. A year is, similarly, the period it takes for the Earth to complete an orbit of the Sun. This is the way our self-conscious mind has developed to deal with the sensory input of the manifest world—utilizing classifications and divisions. However, arbitrary classifications based on perceptions are not necessarily the only or even the best way to apprehend reality. It is artificial and falls apart when we are dealing with consciousness. Which of us has not experienced a dream that seemed to last for hours only to awake and find it, in fact, only lasted a few minutes?

Additionally, as several authors have pointed out, the dimension of the present is ever passing. For example, by the time we say "present," it has already slipped into the "past." Some people become imprisoned by the past. They spend their time rehashing and regretting bygone events and decisions. Or, conversely, they relive their triumphs, the so-called "best years of their life." We in fact can't change history, but we can learn from its lessons.

Similarly, some people live always in the "tomorrow" eagerly planning for a time when life will be happier or more abundant. But, as the old saying informs us, "Tomorrow never comes." It is in the future that we plan and fulfill our dreams. But the future is controlled by the decisions we make in the present.

The 6th stage awakens us from the shifting perception of time to the vision of the eternal NOW. For now is, in reality, all we have. This is the moment in eternity.

This stage culminates in the experience that is the immediate precursor of Cosmic Consciousness. Here our consciousness is awakened to the "fourth dimension." This dimension is defined

179

as that which is at right angles to the other three more traditional ones. Our consciousness is liberated from the limited perceptions of three-dimensional consciousness. All of the work of the first five stages gives birth to this regenerated personality.

This liberation naturally leads to the awakening of the powers of the cosmic fire within. Mystics speak of, The Lost Word. This phrase refers to closely guarded, secret techniques of using sound vibrations to stir into activity the inner, spiritual centers, located along the spinal column.

In Theosophical and New Thought literature, we read of the "Voice of the Silence," or the "Music of the Spheres." These passages refer to an experience that heralds the realization that our true Self, the Self who dwells at the center of each of us, is identical with the One Consciousness of the Universe. At this point in the unfoldment process, the Seeker experiences direct Knowing. We "Know" that we are eternal and that the Self dwells in the Now.

The trigger to "knowing" is the Serpent Fire rising through the hollow tube of the spinal cord. When consciously awakened by a spiritual aspirant, as a result of certain meditative or yogic practices, the cells blocking this channel are actually burned away by the Kundalini. Some seekers ill-advisedly concentrate directly on this area in an attempt to force activations. This practice is extremely dangerous and can lead to insanity.

However, by using the techniques developed by enlightened mystics and esoteric fraternities, the awakening of this power or nerve current may be accomplished safely.

At the core of these techniques is the realization that it is the higher Self, working within the seeker, directs this awakening, causing the subtle nerve current to rise up through the spinal channel until it awakens the center in the brain associated with the pineal gland. Consciousness then emerges into the supersensory dimension described before.

The result of this experience is a shift of identity. We move from the doer of the personality, to the true Self within. The Self is omniscient for the process of illumination and thus the true guide.

Chapter 43: Light in Extension

The seventh stage of unfoldment is called Cosmic Consciousness. Attainment of this stage confers perfect health and radiant well-being. This state of radiant health is contagious. It lifts the awareness of all who come into contact.

And, make no mistake, many have experienced this stage. It is not rare, but also not common. Those who truly have achieved Cosmic Consciousness testify to it by example rather than by proclaiming it loudly.

To experience Cosmic consciousness is to experience a state of realization beyond thought. It is a direct realization of the One Unity in which all sense of separation is erased. It is a realization of the eternity of existence without the need of the filter of our ordinary consciousness with its sense of past, present, and future. In it we become one with the eternal moment of NOW.

It is the ultimate location story—to fully understand it, you have to be there.

When we attain this state on the Path of Return, we will completely understand another's description even though words are inadequate to express this realization.

Living in this realization of oneness is the true goal of all religions and philosophies. Beside this reality, all dogmas, creeds, and precepts are seen for what they are; inadequate substitutions for the experience of the ultimate.

Yet the Adepts who have attained this stage of unfoldment will refrain from casting condemnation on another's form of religious belief. They realize that, for that person, at their particular stage of awakening, it is one attempt to define the indefinable. Their creed, if based on the teachings of one who has had a genuine, inner experience, is simply a tool that will aid them on the Path.

The experience is not in the least hazy or undefined. It is not a "New Age fuzzy nothingness." It is crystal clear in all its details. My teacher once defined it as being in all places, all at once, in all times, all at the same time.

The problem, however, is that our common, ordinary language was designed to convey common, ordinary shared experience. It did not develop in an attempt to convey mystical realizations and is, therefore, inadequate for this task.

The sincere aspirant then is content to find the Path, with the aid of a few road signs provided by those who have gone before, and walk the way him or herself.

I'm continually amazed by how many students are content to simply read books describing "the way." They become very adept at parroting very complex metaphysical theory. But theory does not equal practice. These "arm chair mystics," must reflect on their behavior. No matter how many cookbooks you read, your hunger will remain unsatisfied until you get into the kitchen and prepare the meal.

To emphasize, once again, human self-consciousness should not be denigrated. It is a critical component in the quest for Cosmic Consciousness. Nature cannot produce this stage of unfoldment by itself. As the ancient alchemists inform us, "Nature unaided always fails." However, Nature has spent hundreds of thousands of years developing us to be self-conscious channels of creation; to the aim that we can modify natural conditions and adapt them as co-creators in order to finish the process of awakening to Cosmic Consciousness.

It is the vehicle of our self-conscious directing nature that will transport us from bondage to that state beyond thought. We do not attain consciousness of the cosmic by violating the Law, but by fulfilling it.

It states in the Bible, "Flesh and blood cannot inherit the Kingdom." It is by following the steps laid down by the practical mystics of the past that we transmute our physical and mental bodies into instruments for interacting with the Divine. When the Serpent Fire is aroused, it burns the barriers away and activates the inner nerve centers associated with what in the East are called Chakras. Transformation of certain cell groups are organized into a definite form and function. Gradually, with this change of structure comes a corresponding change in consciousness. New realizations are unveiled that facilitate the birth of a new body, "changed in the twinkling of an eye," or "The New Jerusalem."

It is in this state of unfoldment that the spiritual aspirant's actions become like a dancer, moving gracefully, closely following the steps of the dance; but, conversely being at one with the freedom and ecstasy of it all. At this stage, our consciousness has transmuted our perception from the illusion presented to us, to the vision of reality that flows through us.

PART IV

The Three Grades of the Adept

Chapter 44: Introduction

Both the Eastern and the Western Esoteric Traditions agree that enlightenment is reached by three distinct stages. At each stage, a specific realization has to be attained and manifested. In the East these stages are known as:

1. turiyati chetana – or Cosmic Consciousness;

2. bhagavad chetana – or God Consciousness;

3. brahmi chetana – Unity Consciousness

In the Western Tradition these are known as the Grades of Adeptship:

1. Adeptus Minor or Lesser Adept;

2. Adeptus Major or Greater Adept; and,

3. Adeptus Exemptus or Exempt Adept.

We will examine each of these in turn.

Chapter 45: The Grades of Lesser Adept

The stage of enlightenment designated in the west as Lesser Adept (Adeptus Minor) is associated with the Sephirah Tiphareth on the Qabalistic Tree of Life. Additionally, this grade is assigned to the sixth statement in the Pattern on the Trestle Board, which states:

"In all things great and small, I see the Beauty of the Divine Expression."

When we awaken to this stage, we "perceive the harmonious unity of all consciousness." It has been described as the "music of the spheres" and "the cosmic dance." All descriptions of this realization agree that the One Reality is one of perfect balance, proportion, and harmony.

This stage of the Adeptus Minor receives the Qabalistic title, The Mediating Intelligence, in recognition of the fact that the Individuality or Higher Self functions as the indispensable link in the creative process between the levels higher than humanity and the vast levels of nature.

Tiphareth is positioned halfway between Kether and Malkuth on the middle pillar of consciousness. It is the task of self-consciousness to act as an equilibrating influence in order to mediate the "above" with the "below." It is the destiny of humanity to "redeem" the entire garden. As Jesus states,

"If I be lifted up I shall lift all others unto myself."

The role of redeemer is one that humanity is destined to achieve, not only for itself, but also for the entire life-wave. But to achieve this task humanity must first be awakened. Alchemists, as we have previously emphasized, have a saying:

"Nature unaided always fails."

This teaching is often misunderstood. It does not mean that nature does not fulfill its role. Instead, it refers to a task that the subconscious levels of life were never designed to fulfill. It is the self-conscious mode of human consciousness that modifies, extends, and mediates the natural evolution of life adapting and transforming it to a new paradigm—a higher expression.

It is by preparing, equilibrating, and transforming our natural vehicles that creates the Holy Grail that, in turn, can be filled by the higher awareness of Cosmic Consciousness. This experience of grace is a gift of the Individuality and carries with it the certain, positive conviction of the individual's immortality. This is not merely an intellectual conception, (although that is the first step), but a direct knowingness of this fact.

This awakening is a direct result of the shift of personal identity from the personality to that of the Higher Self. It is a recognition that our consciousness, that which gives us identity, far from originating in our brain, in reality flows through us from a higher source.

At this stage, there is an identity shift from the ever-transitioning activity of the outer to the stable, unmoving, inner, spiritual reality. We recognize the fact of human immortality, and the true democracy and brotherhood/sisterhood of humanity. The unity of all as the basis of our identity is the realization of the Consciousness of the Cosmic.

Chapter 46: The Grade of Major Adept—God Consciousness

This stage of enlightenment is assigned to the fifth Sephirah, Geburah, on the Qabalistic Tree of Life. It should be noted that we do not ascend to the levels above Tiphareth, but rather open ourselves up to their mystical influence. Their knowledge is filtered down into our awareness while centered in the consciousness of our Higher Self.

Geburah is intimately connected with The Law of Response symbolized in the Major Arcana of the Tarot by the ninth trump, The Hermit. This law may be summarized as follows:

All activities in our personal sphere of sensation have their origin in the root cause of the Universe.

Jesus stated, "Of myself, I can do nothing. It is the Father within me who doeth all things." In Key 9, The Hermit, we see a white-bearded ancient, standing in deep contemplation on a mountaintop. He holds high the Lantern of Illumination as a beacon for those struggling up the path below, showing them the way as he witnesses their progress to the height.

The Greater Adept, or one manifesting God-consciousness, embodies the mystery of Free Will. Clerics and laity use this concept of free will, usually misunderstood, to explain various imperfections they perceive in the Divine Plan. They claim because of the exercise of this faculty humankind has "fallen" from grace. In actuality, it is perhaps the opposite that is true. The Divine Plan has no imperfections. It is our perception that is at fault.

This misperception is based on judging an operation *in process* as the finished product. An uncooked pizza should not be used to evaluate the tastiness of the served product. A toddler who stumbles and falls should not discourage the development of the Olympic athlete hidden within, only to emerge in the future after years of discipline training. At every stage of the journey, perfection is manifested. It is only our limited vision that hides this fact from our realization.

The realization of "God-consciousness" reveals the fallacy of free will at the level of personality. When we think of ourselves as the personality, with its shifting, changing components, we have no free will. Our actions and motivations at the level of Greater Adept level become expressions of a stream of causation that unites all people and links them to the Primal Will. All personal activity, at all times and places, is one with this originating principle. True, each individual is a unique and highly specialized expression of this one purpose, but never does any action or volition originate with a personality or individual. The Greater Adept realizes, accepts and practices, day-by-day Jesus' admonition: "Not my will, but Thine be done."

Because of these repeated acts of attention to this indwelling principle the Greater Adept's intuitional capacity becomes highly developed. He continually seeks the guidance of the Inner Teacher.

Alchemically, the blood chemistry of the Adept changes by utilization of the specialized current of the Solar Energy bringing about regeneration and the secret of perpetual youth. The Major Adept consciously transforms the One Power flowing through him. This force that would disintegrate the personality vehicle of an individual of lesser attainment is possible because, having overcome the delusion of a separate personality, he has become proficient in the discipline of balancing the currents flowing through his body; he walks the path of equilibrium. He has realized in every sense of the word that his personality is one with the Cosmic Life Power. He has resolved the existential duality of existence.

Chapter 47: The Grade of Exempt Adept—
Unity Consciousness

Whereas the grade of Greater Adept is concerned with the expression of Cosmic Will, the Exempt Adept expresses the consciousness of Unity; the expression of unconditional, unlimited love. The love that sees accurately all short comings and all "sins" yet still accepts the perfection of that expression.

From what is an Exempt Adept indeed exempt? One answer is the least delusion of separateness. No longer is the consciousness of one simply aware of the cosmic flow expressing through her. Now she completely identifies with that flow. The universal expression of Unity is identified as *her* identity. Hence, she is one with the cosmic power of Love. As explained in Part I, this unity and love are expressed in the Qabalah by the words Achad, (unity) and Ahevah (love).

In the grade of Adeptus Major we experience Cosmic Will and Justice. In this grade of Adeptus Exemptus we experience Love and Compassion. Paul Case repeatedly pointed out that the power to pardon is given only to the governor or ruler. A judge must administer the sentence within the boundaries of the Law.

The Sephirah Chesed, assigned to this grade, is said to be the level of the Chasidim or "Compassionate Ones." These are the Qabalistic saints who become instruments of expression of Universal Love.

The True Rosicrucians took as their seal the initials R and C. This spells out the Hebrew word "Roak," which translates as compassion. Thus the hallmark of a true Adept has always been compassion. With this awareness of Unity, all perceptions of lack, inadequacy, and limitation vanish. An Exempt Adept becomes a vehicle for the "inexhaustible riches of the Limitless Substance."

These realizations represent a full maturing of the enlightenment process. The One Identity triumphs victoriously over the perceived limitation of space and time. An infinite consciousness is expressed. There is no enemy. There is only the Unity. All previously perceived opposites with their delusionary conflicts are transcended. As Patanjali states in his *Yoga Sutras* (chapter 6, verse 29),

"He whose self is based in Unity, whose vision is everywhere is even, sees the Self in all things and all things in the Self.

Chapter 48: The Three Great Truths

About 80 miles North of Los Angeles The Crotona Institute, a world-renowned center of the Theosophical Society, is located in a large park-like setting among the beautiful hills of Ojai. Secluded among its trees and rolling lawns, this quiet yet vibrant spiritual center offers a temple, library, bookstore, and beautiful gardens all of which are perfect for meditation. While I am not a member of the Society, I have on several occasions visited Crotona and enjoyed their serene hospitality.

During one of my visits, I had a long discussion with one of the resident librarians. We discussed the three great lies and how they must be overcome before spiritual enlightenment can be realized. At one point, she looked intently into my eyes and asked if I had ever heard of the Three Great Truths? I admitted that I had not. She pointed to the front rose garden and said that if I walked to the center, I would find a plaque on which was written these truths. I immediately walked to the rose garden and stood gazing down at the following inscriptions.

"The Soul of Man is immortal and is a future of a thing whose growth and splendor have no limit.

"The Principle which gives Life dwells inside us, is undying and eternally beneficent: is not heard or seen or smelt but is perceived by the man who desires such Perception in earnest.

"Each man is his own absolute law-giver, the dispenser of glory or gloom to himself, the decreer of his life, his reward, his punishment.

"These Truths, which are as great as Life itself, are as simple as the mind of man. Feed the hungry with them."

Nothing new, but so profound; a thrill ran through my soul as the import of each of these statements echoed in my mind. Truly these words are food for the spirit—food with which we are being directed to feed the hungry. This food nourishes and transforms society and the family of humanity by transforming and nourishing the individual. The quest of the aspirant is the quest for this transformation; a transformation that is initiated by the seeds planted in the deep consciousness by the contemplation of these great truths.

Chapter 49: Transformation

The Quest for the Holy Grail, the confection of the Philosopher's Stone, is the mystery of the transformation of the personality in its mission to reach its potential and express itself as the One Self. It is the self-re-creation of the vehicles of expression by the Self, that is, the Individuality. This process involves a realization of the unity of life, the foundation of all higher mystical realizations. This is the sum and purpose of the conscious evolutionary process known as Initiation. In the words of T.S. Elliot,

> "We shall not cease from exploration, and
> the end of our exploring will be to arrive
> where we started and know the place for
> the first time."

May Light be extended upon you!

If these teachings have struck a responsive chord in your soul, and you have a genuine desire to serve your fellow humans, by improving yourself in the Mysteries, please visit www.lvx.org for more information. I therefore extend to you a personal invitation to join with us of the Initiated Section to apply for entry into the Temple.

The Fraternity of the Hidden Light is a
world-wide organization working according
to the Pattern of the True and Invisible
Rosicrucian Order with Lodges, Pronaoi, and
Study Groups in major cities around the
globe.

The Steward
c/o The Director of Probationers
P.O. Box 5094, Covina, CA. U.S.A. 91723

*Please visit our website

www.lvx.org

"May you dwell beneath the shadow of His wings, whose name is Peace."

CPSIA information can be obtained
at www.ICGtesting.com
Printed in the USA
FSOW01n1008250217
31266FS